A Short Guide to Writing about Social Science

A SHORT GUIDE TO WRITING ABOUT SOCIAL SCIENCE

■ ■ ■

Fourth Edition

LEE CUBA
Wellesley College

New York   Boston   San Francisco
London   Toronto   Sydney   Tokyo   Singapore   Madrid
Mexico City   Munich   Paris   Cape Town   Hong Kong   Montreal

Vice President/Editor-in-Chief: Joseph Terry
Acquisitions Editor: Susan Kunchandy
Executive Marketing Manager· Carlise Paulson
Supplements Editor. Donna Campion
Senior Production Manager: Eric Jorgensen
Project Coordination, Text Design, and Electronic Page Makeup: UG / GGS
    Information Services, Inc.
Cover Design Manager: John Callahan
Cover Photo Teofilo Olivieri, courtesy of Images com
Senior Manufacturing Buyer Dennis J Para
Printer and Binder: R. R Donnelley & Sons Co
Cover Printer. The Lehigh Press, Inc

For permission to use copyrighted material, grateful acknowledgment is made to the copyright holders on pp 229–230, which are hereby made part of this copyright page

Library of Congress Cataloging-in-Publication Data

Cuba, Lee J.
   A short guide to writing about social science / Lee Cuba -- 4th ed.
      p cm. -- (The short guide series)
Includes bibliographical references and index.
   ISBN 0-321-07842-X (alk. paper)
   1. Social sciences--Authorship. 2. English language--Technical
English. 1 Title.
   H91 .C78 2001
   808' 0663--dc21

                                          2001038246

Please visit our website at http://www.ablongman.com

ISBN 0-321-07842-X

1 2 3 4 5 6 7 8 9 10—DOC—04 03 02 01

CONTENTS

■ ■ ■

PREFACE

∎ ∎ ∎

The fourth edition of this book endeavors to reinforce the main purpose of such a text: to create an approachable guide that illustrates writing in the social sciences without becoming overly cumbersome or so specialized that it becomes promptly outdated. I have attempted to carefully augment what is already a most impressive book by Lee Cuba, contributing insights from my contrasting backgrounds as an English teacher and more recently a professor of international relations. The book aims to give enough guidance to avoid major pitfalls while suggesting where to look for more in-depth information when necessary, such as the evolving debate on citing electronic sources. Many instructors complain that their students cannot effectively write or engage in research. This book can give that help, and moreover is designed not only for students in an introductory course, but also for advanced undergraduate and for beginning graduate students. It therefore has useful reminders for more advanced practitioners: For instance, do they periodically evaluate the success of their writing routine? This volume, an attempt to heal the rift between undergraduate and professional writing, explains how writing fits into each level of academic achievement. Finally, the new checklists at the end of each chapter remind writers of some basics in writing and research at each stage of the process.

Chapter 1 reinforces instruction on writing that students may have had in high school or in a first-year college course. After much

consultation with students over the years, I have found that too many never received even basic writing advice, and need assistance in the crucial step from research to initial writing. The goal is to make these assignments not only less painful, but even transformational for students; clear writing is evidence of knowledge about oneself as well as the subject at hand. It is more than just a skill for future success.

Chapter 2 updates advice on the Internet and some of the benefits and pitfalls of this medium. In giving recommendations on this evolving subject, I intend to give a general framework of assistance, for overly specific guidance can become rapidly obsolete. Today's search engines may not exist tomorrow. I have also attempted to give more direction to beginning researchers, explaining, for example, that some sources they may find may be too specialized but that understanding how to search will bring them to accessible materials. I remember how intimidated I was in my first university year by the materials in the library, so I have attempted to assuage similar fears in undergraduates when confronting the much larger amount of material today.

Chapters 3 through 6 illustrate diverse types of writing, and speaking, in social science. In these chapters, I have attempted again to explain more basically the terminology and procedures of different types of research and to explain them more thoroughly to the beginning researcher. Hopefully this section will prove useful to instructors in bringing students into their discipline, knowledge I certainly could have used both as an undergraduate and graduate student. I have included suggestions made by reviewers of earlier editions and drafts, such as discussing contrasting structures for papers and augmenting the chapter on writing library research papers, the most common type for undergraduates. As I teach several courses with a strong oral component, I have added a number of suggestions in Chapter 6 of use to both students and professionals.

Chapter 7 broadens the discussion of documentation forms by explaining more explicitly the different citation styles, which are evolving in each social science, but also by explaining basic com-

monalities between them. There are many detailed manuals on the individual forms both in print and on the Internet; this guide is alternatively intended to get students on the right path without frantically consulting many complicated pages. Here again, I try to lessen the gap between the academic preparing to submit to a specialized journal and the undergraduate composing a paper early in their social science major, or more terrifyingly, in an elective.

Last, again following the suggestions of helpful reviewers, I emphasize the need for sustained and thoughtful revision, something I believe current university students have the most difficulty doing. Certainly most writers understand their mistakes after an editor or professor returns work; the secret is to make them return to their manuscript frequently enough to identify and repair these errors before submission. As in other creative acts, such as sculpture or architecture, the final ten percent of perfecting the work is everything in terms of avoiding blemishes that diminish the entire effort.

I have contributed modestly to an already amazingly useful text by Lee Cuba. I wish to thank him for his confidence and patience in me and hope my ideas are considered a complement to his previous hard work. Thanks also to the reviewers of the manuscript; I have attempted to include many of your thoughtful suggestions. I am furthermore extremely indebted to Winthrop University students and professionals who have helped me in this book: Susan Silverman and Lois Walker of the library; Dr. Douglas Eckberg, Dr. Jennifer Solomon, and Dr. Jonathan Marx of the Sociology Department; Dr. Jeffrey Sinn of the Psychology Department; Dr. Hannah Britton and Dr. Karen Kedrowski of the Political Science Department; Dr. Lynne Dunne and Dr. David Pretty of the History Department; Dr. Gloria Jones, Dr. Jo Tarvers, and Evelyne Weeks of the English Department and the Writing Center; and Suzanne Smith and Stan Hulon, two sterling student assistants. Finally I want to thank the kind editors at Longman, who waited so patiently for the final product.

CHRIS VAN ALLER

THE PRACTICE OF WRITING

■ ■ ■

Social scientists write about the methods they use to collect and analyze social data, and they write about the results these methods yield. But social scientists have seldom examined the practice of writing itself and its relation to the process of research. As a result, students in the social sciences see or understand little of what happens between the collection of data and the publication of research results. *A Short Guide to Writing about Social Science* focuses on this critical omission by taking a serious look at the practice of social science writing. As a key bonus, learning to communicate your thoughts effectively in writing will enable you to learn to think more carefully and to learn in an active way.

Effective writing—about any subject—requires practice. In one sense (as in "practice makes perfect"), practice means repeated writing, editing, and rewriting, thereby sharpening our words so that we express our ideas clearly to our audience. Repeated writing of almost any kind has a cumulative effect, in the sense that practice conquers fear and contributes to greater productivity in shorter periods of time. Writing instructors often have their students use journals, in which students react to readings or life experiences, because they contribute to writing facility in an enjoyable way. In this sense, putting pen to paper or fingers to keys is like practicing a musical instrument; many great writers hone their craft in letters and diaries.

However, writing can also be thought of as a practice in a different sense (as in "medical practice"), as a complex of routines we develop around the act of writing. These routines reflect our assumptions about the nature of creative thought, as well as our superstitions about our own success or failure as writers. All great writers have their creative routines, such as writing in the morning or for most of the night, in a creative pattern that works for them. For their part, many undergraduates believe that writing a term paper is a mechanistic task comprising a series of long-understood and definite steps: One chooses a topic, then compiles a bibliography, collects intimidating amounts of information on large stacks of index cards, writes an elaborate outline, and finally, writes the paper. As suggested by certain writing manuals, writing begins only *after* all of the necessary research is done and the argument is well organized. The first draft of the paper, according to this perspective, involves nothing more than methodically writing down what has been carefully planned beforehand; some authorities say the first draft almost "writes itself." Creativity enters into this process only in deciding *how* to say what we have discovered, not in determining *what* to say.

Students who hold this misconception about the writing process often put off writing until the paper is fully outlined and developed, or until time has run out, and the sun is rising over the computer after the all nighter. Inadequacies or shortcomings of the paper are, therefore, typically attributed to insufficient time. The irony of conceiving of writing as the grand conclusion to weeks of research is that it serves as a deterrent to writing in the first place. Graduate students in particular are guilty of taking refuge in endless research to avoid the actual writing of their thesis until the deadline is imminent. Thinking that we must know exactly what we are going to say before we begin writing can create a "writer's block" of seemingly insurmountable proportions.

To define writing as simply communicating ideas *to others* fails to account for the fact that, in writing, we communicate something *to ourselves*. When we write a paper or even a sentence, we *objectify* our thoughts. Through writing, our thoughts are separated from us, assuming an existence and a nature of their own. You have no doubt experienced this process yourself, although you may not have thought of it in these terms. Have you ever reread a paper or a letter you wrote months or years ago? If you have, you may have been amazed that what you wrote what you are reading. And depending on what you read, your reaction may have ranged from embarrassment to pride. The necessity of getting away from one's work is absolute; it is often amazing how different your writing appears after as little as one day away.

My point is that when we read such a paper or letter, we are forced to confront and experience the objective reality of our words, as occasionally painful as this act can be! Of course, months or years need not elapse before we come to see our writing as distinct from ourselves. The minute we write a sentence we may realize that it does not express what we want to say, or (even more often) that it does express what we *did have* to say, but we now see we have a better idea. We write, "There are two reasons why . . . ," and our mind, racing ahead, suddenly realizes we are thinking of *three* reasons, or, on the other hand, that one of our two reasons is not much of a reason and therefore not worth stating. This process of simultaneous thought and revision is made even more efficient as we now write on computers; rapid change is effortless, and certainly less wasteful of paper.

Thus, writing provides a constant opportunity to deepen our understanding and sharpen our insights. Taking advantage of this opportunity requires that writing be followed by revising and rewriting to reflect on these insights. What we call "writing" might better be called "rewriting" or "revising." Think of writing as a process— not an outcome—involving an ongoing dialogue with ourselves and with our imagined readers. In a sense you, become your own editor; a more objective and distant being who points out problems and makes suggestions. As we organize observations, fashion arguments, and articulate conclusions, new ideas will emerge that we could never have anticipated initially. Writing, an analytically creative task, is a necessary part of social research. This means that writing, like the methods of social research, can help us to learn more about social life.

To recognize that writing is an analytic strategy that you can develop with practice, you must adopt certain attitudes toward writing as a practice. This perspective on writing frees you from the burden of developing a tight-knit argument before you commit your thoughts to paper. It implies that your first draft will not (or more to the point, cannot) be your final product. Writing will become less painful and more productive as you design the routines that work for you. Only after you begin to write your paper, essay, or examination will you know what you want to say, and you will almost surely find that your idea of what you want to say develops as you write it. Learning to perfect your writing will help you in any career field; even composing effective letters of application (large corporations receive thousands per week) demands this sort of active writing strategy.

Taking revision to heart means that you must be willing to part with your words. It is not unusual for practiced writers to labor over a paragraph or a page, only to realize later that those carefully crafted words must be discarded. Less experienced authors become so enamored of a perfect sentence or expression that the revision process is incomplete. Being wedded to a single expression of your ideas not only ignores the emergent nature of writing, it also thwarts your understanding of what you are trying to write about.

Second, viewing your words as separate from yourself helps you to accept constructive criticism of your writing. It is easy to regard editorial criticism as a personal attack on your character, indicative of some intellectual flaw All writers feel slightly anxious while watching someone read their work. Of course, you would welcome a little praise from others for what you write, but you should also realize that critical revision of your writing can only strengthen your argument. Incorporating the constructive criticism of others gives you an additional chance to "get it right." For those who feel diminished by criticism, keep in mind that editorial remarks are directed at your paper, not at you.

Third, developing the editorial skills necessary to critique the work of others will help you to identify problems in your own writing. Students and professors who are perceptive editors of the writing of others usually can identify the weaknesses of their own writing and know how to revise it. That is, they can objectify their own writing, as well as the writing of others. It is initially much easier to see the mistakes of others, particularly one's peers. This in turn teaches you to identify your problems, ones otherwise repeated in paper after paper.

When other people read a paper you have written, they can assess your argument only in terms of what appears before them. In this sense writing is very different from speaking, with its gestures and intonations. It may not help you to read your paper out loud to yourself or someone else. Your audience cannot be expected to know the unstated information and understandings—the thinking, outlining, research, writing, and rewriting—that preceded this draft of your paper. As authors, we know what we meant, and consequently we may mistakenly assume that our readers simply must understand the thoughts behind the words. Learning to distance yourself from your writing is an important first step in acquiring the skills of self-editing. I discuss how to accomplish this later in this chapter, but first let's turn to an example of how revision can act to create insights, as well as to sharpen existing ideas.

WRITING, EDITING, AND RETHINKING: AN EXAMPLE

The best way to discover how editing and rewriting can improve your writing is to trace their evolution through a series of drafts. To illustrate this process, I have chosen a paragraph embedded in a much longer text that, after several revisions, was incorporated into a journal-length article. (In attempting to follow my advice regarding editorial openness, I present an example from my own writing.) A single isolated paragraph, of course, cannot reveal how material from disparate sections of the original text was eventually reorganized to form the smaller article; nevertheless, it does show you how one largely descriptive paragraph can form the basis of a more insightful analysis.

Here is the first draft of the paragraph:

DRAFT 1 (ORIGINAL)

Learning to talk "like an Alaskan" is an important part of becoming an Alaskan. It is one's claim to membership, a part of the frontier experience. Noticeably, residents of Anchorage do not refer to themselves as "Anchoragites" but as "Alaskans." Identification with the state rather than the city is strong, an obvious point to those who have seen the sprawl of urban Anchorage. Thus, the majority of the words unique to Alaska are descriptive of the region, rather than the city itself. Examples include: Outside; Cheechako; Sourdough; cabin fever. Most others have something to do with the weather. Placing bets on the dates of "freeze up" and "break up" are annual events, as is speculation over when the "termination dust" (first snow of the season) will arrive. "White out" is not something a secretary uses but is a hazardous condition caused by "ice fog" in which light reflects off the snow yet casts no shadow. A "cache" used to be a place where food was stored out of the reach of wild animals: today it refers to a business and is often preceded by the appropriate product name, as in The Book Cache, The Stamp and Coin Cache. Though many of the cruder elements of early Alaska have vanished from the streets of downtown Anchorage, the region's frontier history lives on in daily conversation.

This paragraph can be improved in specific and creative ways, and here again, coming back to the work later made this process possible. After rereading it several times, I decided that the paragraph was weak in at least three areas. First, it is plagued with imprecise language. Take, for example, the first sentence: "Learning to talk 'like an Alaskan' is an important part of becoming an Alaskan." What does it mean to describe something as "an important part"? (Do "unimportant" issues have a place in our writing?) What if I instead wrote; "Learning to talk 'like an Alaskan' is the first step in becoming an Alaskan"? The revised sentence leads the reader to anticipate a discussion of further stages in the process of achieving a new identity, thus lending a temporal element to the writing and preparing for the future continuity of the piece.

Second, as it stands, this paragraph assumes that my readers have a good deal of background information about my topic. By failing to define "Outside," "Cheechako," "Sourdough," and "cabin fever," I weaken my claim that contemporary Alaskan dialogue is grounded in the imagery of its frontier history. The reader will be thrown back onto his or her knowledge of such terms, gleaned from a host of disparate sources (perhaps western movies). Yet social science uses terms in definite ways, separate from their meaning in everyday discourse. More on this key point will follow in Chapter 2.

Third, I seem to be trying to cram too much material into one place. Rereading with an eye toward clarity and organization, I decided that the original paragraph could be meaningfully divided into two because many of the examples at the end of the passage deal with the importance of climate to early Alaskan life; these examples describe things, not people. The first part of the original paragraph, by contrast, focuses on how Alaskans use a frontier vocabulary to distinguish themselves from others.

In dividing the material in the original draft into two paragraphs, I was making an *analytical* judgment. *Analysis* involves breaking down something into parts or categories in attempting to understand what that something is and how the pieces relate to each other. In this example, I am trying to show the significance of a particular regional vocabulary as it is used to describe two groups: people and things.

Making these changes, I felt, took several steps in improving this passage. My revision of the original paragraph read as follows (changes from the first draft have been underlined):

DRAFT 2

Learning to talk "like an Alaskan" is <u>the first step</u> in becoming an Alaskan. It is one's claim to membership, <u>an integral</u> part of the frontier experience. Noticeably, residents of Anchorage do not refer to themselves as "Anchoragites" but as "Alaskans." Identification with the state rather than the city is strong <u>for reasons obvious</u> to those who have seen the <u>urban sprawl</u> of Anchorage. Thus, the majority of the words unique to Alaska are descriptive of the region, rather than the city itself. <u>Most frequently heard is the term "Outside," which refers to any place which is not Alaska. Newcomers are called "Cheechakos" and old-timers "Sourdoughs," both linguistic vestiges from the days of the Alaska gold rush. The former is a derivative of "Chicago" and connotes the inexperience often displayed by newcomers to Alaska. A Sourdough, on the other hand, was a veteran prospector, the name coming from the type of bread carried on the trail.</u>

<u>Several other such characterizations have their origin in earlier times when climate played a major role in affecting the course of Alaskan life. The restless, claustrophobic feeling which accompanies the long hours of winter darkness is familiarly known as "cabin fever."</u> Placing bets on the dates of "freeze up" and "break up" are annual events, as is speculation over when the "termination dust" (first snow of the season) will arrive. "White out" is not <u>an office supply</u> but a hazardous condition caused by "ice fog" in which light reflects off the snow <u>casting</u> no shadow. A "cache" used to be a place where food was stored out of the reach of wild animals; today it <u>usually</u> refers to a business and is often preceded by the appropriate product name—<u>hence</u>, The Book Cache, The

Stamp and Coin Cache. Though many of the cruder
elements of early Alaska have vanished from the
streets of downtown Anchorage, <u>a part of its</u>
history lives on in daily conversation.

Thinking that the paper was ready for an outsider to read, I asked one of my colleagues to edit it. When she returned the paper a few days later, she asked me what the point of it was. Somewhat surprised, I replied that these paragraphs concerned how a nineteenth century frontier vocabulary could be refashioned to describe a twentieth-century experience. Wasn't that obvious from what I had written?

After a lengthy discussion with my friend, it became clear that I had not seriously asked myself *what* the theme of these paragraphs was. As I reread what I had written, I began to consider what these many examples from Alaska said about more general questions of language and its role in attaching people to communities. Instead of concentrating on Alaska, I began to ask, "How does this example relate to our understanding of basic social processes?" The first two sentences of the original draft hinted at the relationship between language and community membership, but this idea remained undeveloped even in the revision.

In short, the problem with the second revision was that it provided a lot of evidence but failed to make a general point. The paragraphs were primarily descriptive lists of colorful Alaskan words and phrases. Were all of these examples alike? Did my method of analysis need to be changed—that is, could these examples be organized thematically, in a more meaningful way? In working through such questions, I was forced to confront the weaknesses of my previous analytical strategies. My revisions were now leading me toward a deeper understanding of the issues embodied in these specific illustrations gathered from my fieldwork in Alaska. I was ferreting out the ideas that were in my subconscious, sequencing them and expanding on their meaning. In this sense, clear writing calls forth an increased understanding of the subject at hand. This continual return and reevaluation of writing is hard work, but there is no substitute if you want a reasoned and insightful paper.

Rethinking and revising the second draft resulted in expanding the previous two paragraphs into six. Presented here is the third draft, in a slightly abbreviated version (as before, the revised text has been underlined):

DRAFT 3

One of the fundamental institutions which facilitates group identification is language. In acquiring the language of the group, new arrivals not only come to view themselves as group members, but they also become participants in the "symbolic environment" of the group (Shibutani 1961:490). Adoption of a common dialect, then, implies identification with the group's history and a shared perception of the group's location in social and cultural space. As Mills (1939:677) writes:

> Along with language, we acquire a set of social norms and values. A vocabulary is not merely a string of words; immanent within it are societal textures—institutional and political coordinates. Back of every vocabulary lie sets of collective action.

Residents of Anchorage, like those living in other regions of the country, employ a vernacular unique to their surroundings, and learning to "talk like an Alaskan" is the first step in becoming an Alaskan. The evaluative statements implicit in the regional vocabulary of Anchorage residents express three themes: a distinction between those living in Alaska and those living in other areas of the country; a distinction among groups of state residents; and an identification with the state as a whole, rather than with Anchorage itself—a distinction which emphasizes the more primitive side of Alaskan life. One of the first things newcomers to Alaska notice is that virtually all Alaskans refer to nonresidents as "Outsiders" and to any place which is not Alaska as "Outside." These labels which boast connotations of state chauvinism form a part of everyday conversation and act as continual reminders that others know very little about Alaska and its ways. Comments like "Outsiders have no way of knowing what we're like" are not infrequently voiced, as local residents are quick to stress the importance of having lived in the state as a necessary precondition to forming opinions about Alaskans.

In a similar manner language becomes a vehicle for marking differences between those who merely reside in the state and those who are "real Alaskans." The former are called "Cheechakos" and the latter "Sourdoughs," both linguistic vestiges from the days of the Alaska gold rush. "Cheechako" is a derivative of "Chicago" and refers to the inexperience displayed by newcomers to Alaska. A "Sourdough," on the other hand, was a veteran prospector, the name coming from the bread carried on the trail. Because these two terms connote achieved status differences, the words of old-timers are sometimes used to legitimate the claims of individuals or organizations.

Significantly, local residents do not refer to themselves as "Anchoragites" for reasons obvious to those who have seen the urban sprawl of Alaska's largest city. A city of 200,000, Anchorage has been alternately portrayed as the "American nightmare" by Norman Mailer and as an "instant Albuquerque" by John McPhee. Yet despite the presence of glass office buildings, paved streets and residential suburbs, the livelier aspects of Alaska's past live on in the daily conversations of Anchorage residents.

Many of these characterizations have their origin in times when climate played a major role in affecting the course of Alaskan life. The restless, claustrophobic feeling which accompanies the long hours of winter darkness is familiarly known as "cabin fever." (Cuba 1984: 222-223)

This third draft, while preserving much of the description found in the original paragraph, is now focused analytically. The general significance of this example has been explained in a new opening paragraph. References to well-known sociologists have been added, establishing a link between the Alaskan example and concepts familiar to a larger professional audience. The language used to express these ideas is also somewhat formal, reflecting my perception of who would be likely to read this article. Whether you write as a student or professor in social science, or you plan to make your living in a social science career such as law enforcement, the necessity of placing analysis and focus above description would remain the goal.

The second paragraph begins with a revised version of the first sentence of the previous draft but is followed by a rather long sentence outlining the organization of the later paragraphs. This organizing scheme is a critical aspect of this draft. It does more than alert the reader to what follows; it provides a thematic guide sorely lacking in the first two versions. The reader must be kept in mind at all times, in terms of making sure they are never lost in the text. The examples that appear in the first draft as a long list of descriptive items are now grouped according to what they reveal about Alaskan life. A few more illustrations have been included, but, for the most part, the remaining paragraphs consist of material reorganized from the earlier drafts. Beginning writers often feel that every sentence must incorporate great masses of data when in fact real analysis of a paper means further elaborating on the material already at hand. Although it may seem that this draft is just a matter of moving sentences from here to there, by developing this framework, this third draft carries the previous drafts beyond description to analysis

This illustration from my writing demonstrates, I hope, the benefits of rewriting as rethinking. My description of the process as it appears here, however, is not entirely accurate. Presenting this example in a neat "one-two-three" draft format misrepresents the practice of writing. Sometimes saving earlier drafts on paper or as a file on your computer can remind you of an approach or idea that may be worth renewed attention. Writing, editing, and rethinking do not form an orderly and one-way enterprise. Changes occur incrementally, new ideas emerge in varied sequence, and few if any of the changes shown here were the product of initial inspiration.

It is similarly misleading to suggest that only two drafts preceded the third draft shown here. I cannot remember exactly how many times I reworked these paragraphs, but I would estimate that I made seven or eight revisions between Draft 1 and Draft 3. That Draft 3 became the "final" draft had more to do with a publication deadline than with the confidence that I had at last gotten it right. All kinds of deadlines—for class projects, for committee reports, for symposium papers—bring closure to our writing. It is our responsibility as writers to allow enough time so that our first is never our final draft. Finally, remember that writing is a voyage of self-discovery, and the journey matters at least as much as the final destination, for writers of every age and occupation.

SOME HINTS ON GETTING STARTED

There is no simple formula for arriving at a writing strategy that yields consistently good results for everyone. There are, nevertheless, some general guidelines you can follow on the way to developing a habit of writing that works best for you.

1. *Describe and assess your current writing habits.* Before you can improve your writing, you must know how you write. Assume the perspective of a social scientist interested in the rituals of writing (Becker 1986), and begin by taking an inventory of your present writing habits. When do you first begin to write an assigned paper or exam? What time of day do you usually write? What kinds of equipment (typewriters, word processors, pen) do you use? How many drafts of a paper do you normally complete before turning it in? Do you revise solely on the computer or make multiple paper drafts?

Where do you write? Do you write in short segments or for long periods at a time? Do you let others read your paper before you complete a last draft? Do you make notes or an outline before you begin to write? How do you assemble material that you will use in your paper? Aim for as complete a description of your writing—the whens, wheres, and hows—as possible, and make notes of your observations.

Next, turn your attention to analyzing these data. Think about which habits produce the best results and which ones create problems: Do your writing habits assume a constant pattern, or do they vary by course, topic, and type of writing? Do some practices consistently lead to trouble, such as failure to meet scheduled deadlines, inability to identify grammatical mistakes, or poor organization? If you take this exercise seriously, not only will you have a better idea of how to improve your writing, but also you will have taken a major step toward demystifying the process of writing. One way of auditing yourself in this manner is to save all your previous papers, from the first year of university on, and write down all the previous mistakes your "editors" have noted in your work. I did this myself at university and consulted my "mistake book" before turning in the last draft of any paper.

2. *Start early.* It is virtually impossible to begin working on a paper too soon. Revisions take a lot of time, and yet they are indispensable if you are going to use the process of writing as a tool for analyzing social life. Once you incorporate revision into your definition of writing an examination (obviously there is less actual rewriting in a class examination), oral presentation, book review, or research paper, and once you see the results, you will find that allowing time for revision is no less important than logging hours in the library for preparing to write. Starting to think and write as soon as possible will tap into the considerable power of the unconscious, and all sorts of ideas will appear in your head unexpectedly. As soon as a project is assigned, begin thinking about how you will approach it. What will be your general topic? What kinds of information could you gather to discuss this topic? Talk about your ideas with your instructor, other people in your class, or your friends. Most important, jot down notes on your ideas

throughout your thought process. Making rough outlines of your topic will provide a foundation for writing later on, and it also gets you into the practice of objectifying (and therefore clarifying) your thoughts.

It does not matter whether you write in a journal, type notes into a word processing file, use one of the new electronic data devices that connect to your PC, or jot down ideas on slips of paper that you store in a shoe box. (I prefer to keep notes in a computer file—words, phrases, sentence fragments—that I can later develop into sentences and paragraphs of the paper.) Just remember to keep your notes, observations, and other research materials in one place. When you sit down to write a draft of your project, you will not be starting cold. Rather, you will find, to your pleasant surprise, that you have been writing all along.

3. *Read with a critical eye.* Every day we read many different kinds of writing—newspapers, magazines, novels, textbooks, and so on. Some we read for pleasure, some because they are required. We skim some and plod through others, but, in general, we think of reading in terms of what substantive information it offers us: a review of a movie we may want to see, an interesting point to pursue in a research paper, a detailed analysis of some public issue. If we find what we read useful or interesting, it is usually because it contains what we were looking for. In short, it fulfills our expectations about *content.*

In contrast, we sometimes find that our interest in what we are reading stems from how it is written. A clever organizing scheme, an unusual choice of words, or an illuminating analogy can appeal to us regardless of content. In these instances we are admiring someone's prowess as a writer. As you read, make it a point to pay close attention to what you like and what you dislike about an author's presentation. Then, try to come up with a reason for *why* you liked or disliked it. In doing so, you will have the opportunity both to learn how others deal with issues of audience, tone, and argumentation and to see whether analogous solutions can be incorporated into your own writing. You will also be on your way to becoming a critical editor.

4. *Learn to write using a word processor or computer.* As a graduate student, I wrote my Ph.D. thesis at a typewriter. Looking back on that experience, I can not remember whether I spent more time composing or cutting and pasting sections of barely legible text. Putting together a readable draft of a chapter could easily consume an entire day, a discouraging task given that each chapter had to be rewritten several times. When my advisors at last assured me that no further revisions were necessary, I had to pay several hundred dollars to have the thesis typed.

For a number of reasons, word processing has transformed the way many of us write. The capabilities of these systems are expanding every day, both in terms of power and ease of use. Words, sentences, and paragraphs can easily be moved within a single document or from one document to another. Clean drafts can be generated whenever they are needed. Complex formatting procedures, such as justification, centering, or footnoting, require only a few keystrokes. Because word processing software often comes with a variety of specialized subprograms, you can also use it to check your manuscript for spelling errors, substitute one word for another using a thesaurus program, or compile a list of references using an appropriate citation style. All of these qualities of word processing facilitate writing and rewriting and increase the likelihood that you will make revisions. Word processing thus affords students and professors the opportunity to exchange writing assignments for reconsideration and revision several times before they are due, without adding the time-consuming burden of retyping each draft. One can even send documents back and forth via e-mail, greatly increasing the interaction of writer and editor. Consequently, I strongly urge you to learn to write on a word processor or computer (if you do not already do so). If at all possible, buy or use the best computer and software available as capabilities will be much greater than cheaper alternatives.

There are people who are intimidated by the computer's growing abilities, yet learning a word processing program is not difficult. And taking time to learn some version of word processing software will help you in any number of situations—courses, research assistantships, jobs—where writing is required. You can learn each system gradually, challenging yourself to master various tools in the program and becoming more efficient. If you have your own computer, you can select any word processing software compatible with your machine. However, if you have yet to purchase any software, it is best to consult the computing staff at your institution to find out which programs they support. (Because of the number of software programs available, many institutions select only one or two for which they will provide training and technical assistance.) Most colleges and universities do not expect all students and staff to own their own machines, so they make word processing software available on their institutional computer systems. If you are not going to purchase your own computer, find out what resources are available at your institution and start using them. It is also true that some software programs are better for some applications, such as presenting data on graphs, than others, so check the benefits of each system. Finally, be aware of the pitfalls of computers, such as your hard drive "crashing," and erasing your manuscript! Computer experts believe in the concept of inverse diminishing probability; what this means is that you have the highest level of back-up capability for those documents and files that are the most important.

5. *Develop your editorial skills.* To reap the benefits of rethinking and rewriting, you must become a good editor. But how do you acquire the necessary skills? Acquiring useful editorial skills takes practice, and there is no single best way to edit a piece of writing. Some people prefer to edit papers line by line, checking each sentence for clarity, conciseness, and grammar. Others prefer to focus on questions of organization, balance, and style as they affect the general shape and content of a paper. Obviously, some combination of these editorial styles will yield the best results. You can find some suggestions concerning both specific and general revisions of paper drafts in Chapter 8.

Bear in mind that writing is a collegial enterprise. Social scientists, from students to professors, read and comment on each other's writing. You may have noticed that authors of books and articles you have encountered in your research usually acknowledge the assistance of others. Some of the editorial insights that emerge in a piece of writing are the author's, some come from other readers, and some—often the most helpful—result from the author's discussion with his or her colleagues. Enlisting the aid of a circle of editorial friends can improve your writing immeasurably. Just remember to return the favor by reading their papers and giving appropriate credit for editorial suggestions that you adopt.

I often find that students are reluctant to discuss class assignments with their friends or to ask their friends to read papers the students have written, fearing that such practices violate codes of academic honesty. (The honor code at my institution tends to reinforce students' perceptions that they must complete course assignments without enlisting the help of their peers.) Although independent effort is expected on individual projects, most professors welcome student editing groups in their classes. If you are worried about your professors' opinions about student editing, discuss this option with them or consult with your university's writing center. Some professors are also willing to review multiple drafts of your paper; these people are indeed saints and their generosity should be utilized whenever possible. And if you intend to incorporate the suggestions of your peer editors—for example, an additional argument you had not considered or a revision of an awkward paragraph—be sure to ask the permission of these editors before you include their contributions in your paper. Then, include a proper acknowledgment for this editorial assistance in a footnote or preface to your paper. If your professor frowns on any outside help on your paper, ask them what sorts of mistakes are common in this type of assignment.

If you are at a more advanced stage of your academic career, and receive an edited copy of your work from a journal, your editor will be quick to indicate specific details about your paper's major weaknesses. Do not feel that you have to accept all of the comments of your editor. Your disagreement with an editor may, in fact, spawn a productive debate about your writing that leads to rethinking and revision in another direction. The primary purpose of editing is to open up a dialogue, not simply to acquiesce to the suggestions of others. If you are editing your own work—and all writers must develop the habit of editing their own work—you need to find ways to distance yourself from your writing. One simple step in that direction involves transferring your writing from one medium to another. Readers, as well as authors, respond quite differently to typewritten, prepublication drafts and printed, published copies of the same material. If you usually draft papers in longhand, try typing them before editing. If your first drafts arise out of interactions with a word processor, make your revisions on a printed copy. Repeated printed copies after each revision will alert you to how your work will appear to others, and provide more emergency backups. "Transcribing" your writing in this manner provides an alternative context for your words that is essential in objectifying your thoughts. Of course, allowing ample time between writing and editing also helps in this process. That is why it is impossible to overstate the need to start writing early.

QUESTIONS ON WRITING

1 Do you write on a regular basis, in a diary or journal for example?

2. Do you prefer prolonging research, only to write the paper at the last minute?

3 Have you understood and internalized the mistakes made on previous papers?

4. Have you evaluated the success or failure of your writing routine?

5. How successful are you at becoming your own editor, at objectively revising your work?

6 Are you aware of the benefits and liabilities of writing with computers?

7 Do you attempt to find others to help you refine your work?

8. Do you transcribe your work into different mediums to enhance detachment?

USING THE LIBRARY AND THE INTERNET

■ ■ ■

No matter what kind of social science writing you do, it will probably require that you devote some time to library research. If you are writing a research paper based partly on work that others have done, you may well spend as much time gathering, reading, and analyzing this literature as you do writing the paper. But even if your writing assignment is confined to materials distributed by an instructor in a course, you may find it helpful to turn to the library for additional source materials—either dictionaries or encyclopedias to define or clarify social science concepts, or supplemental studies to provide a broader context for your paper. Time spent in the library or searching the Internet for scholarly sites is not something you do only *before* you begin to write, it is an integrated part of the process of writing. Many instructors require a bibliography long before the paper is due to ensure appropriate background research in terms of quality and quantity of sources appropriate to the assignment. Moreover, the necessity of early library exploration *to decide on* possible topics is often imperfectly understood; one does not choose a topic without substantial investigation and evaluation of potential materials.

Libraries and library research have changed dramatically in the few years since the first edition of this book was published, largely because computers and computer networks have multiplied the opportunities for exploring knowledge exponentially. Libraries are not just repositories of books, journals, and newspapers; they are gateways that access information on demand, from outside sources as well as from their own collections. Increasingly, texts of articles and documents not owned by a library can be printed out from an Internet site, a taped archive, or a CD-ROM (compact disk—read-only memory). Hundreds of online library catalogs throughout the world can be consulted as needed via the Internet, as well as a host of other social science sources like government records. Students may look at all of these sources via modem from home or student dorm, at any time of day or night, increasing the time available for thorough searching.

All of this means, of course, that your capacity to search for information has been greatly expanded, increasing the likelihood that you can locate relevant materials for a particular paper. However, it also means that you must acquire an understanding of how computer technology is used to expedite bibliographic research, so that you can *control and evaluate* the vast quantities of information these technologies can generate.

This chapter provides a selective overview of the library resources most often used by social scientists, from novice undergraduates to seasoned professors. The specialized dictionaries and encyclopedias, indexes, bibliographies, and journals discussed here are especially useful to anthropologists, sociologists, political scientists, economists, and psychologists. But before examining the details of social science library research, let's consider some broad guidelines that may expedite your search for useful materials.

SOME GENERAL ADVICE

It is important to approach library research with a realistic set of assumptions and expectations. Even a modest institution has an enormous amount of "possibly relevant" material, and computer networks continue to broaden the scope of library searches literally by the hour. It will take time, savvy, concentration, and—yes—even the help of librarians to identify and then get your hands on the specific materials *you* will find useful. You will master these searches over time, even if it seems overwhelming at first. Keeping the following general guidelines in mind may help alleviate the anxiety and needless delays that often accompany researching your paper:

1. *Create a schedule, and stick to it.* Library research, like all other elements of the writing process, is unlike classroom participation. When you attend a class, you probably participate in a plan devised by your instructor, who has organized the hour, but when you go to the library, you must design your own research plan. What makes library research a creative task is also what makes it time consuming. Do not be surprised if the number of hours you spend in the library or at your computer at home is two to three times longer than what you initially expect.

Why does library research take so much time? Some delays result from the need to acquire skills and experience in the use of libraries. Each item is unique and possesses varying relevance for each user. Electronic resources, available locally or on the Internet, change rapidly as technology advances. Libraries, therefore, can never be organized so that bibliographic research will appear simple and straightforward to everyone. Some organizing schemes used by your institution or one continents away will seem logical or intuitive; others will appear overly complicated and intimidating to the inexperienced researcher. Learning how to use your library effectively takes time, energy, and a taste for exploration!

A variety of other distracting events may interrupt your bibliographic research. You may identify a reference to a journal article or book that your library does not own or cannot print out. Your librarian can probably obtain a copy of what you need through cooperative resource sharing or a document delivery service, but there will necessarily be a delay before you receive it. Even when your library possesses a book you need, it may be temporarily on loan to someone else or placed on reserve for intensive use by a particular class. Some Internet sources that used to be free now charge for information, a trend that appears to be growing, and libraries often charge students for copying articles or interlibrary loan, so starting early can also provide ways to conserve your limited funds.

Delays in your research also stem from the emergent nature of the writing process. When you must select your own topic for a paper, your initial time in the library is exploratory, and very little, if any, of your early efforts may contribute directly to your final paper. You may skim or read many books, encyclopedias, and indexes before you find a topic that both interests you and provides sufficient material for analysis. Tracking down and evaluating sources is akin to detective work; the patient gumshoe never knows which clues will lead to a satisfying resolution.

Just as half a day is probably insufficient for bibliographic research, half a term is probably excessive. Library research can easily turn into an exercise that becomes an end in itself, rather than a means to an end. Especially for students, it can provide a tempting rationalization for not writing (e.g., "I don't know enough to start writing yet"). Develop some balance among gathering, analyzing, and writing about library materials. If you are having difficulty knowing how much time is enough, discuss the materials you have located with your instructor. You can always return to the library for additional sources, but you cannot expect to make the best use of what you collect if you are still seeking new material a week before your paper is due. Sometimes simply starting to write by a specific date is helpful, which is also sound advice if you have multiple papers due during the semester. Most of the time you will have more data or material than are needed to start writing. As detailed in Chapter 1, you need to start writing as soon as possible to explain and debate the meaning of what you have to yourself, to begin the creative dialogue.

2. *Keep a careful record of your library research.* Because it is often impossible to know exactly what materials will be helpful in writing your final paper, keeping track of what you read can save time later on. Documenting your search need not entail writing detailed summaries of everything, but you should at least make brief notes of materials you find. Be sure to include information on how

to relocate these materials; call numbers of books are a must, as are the volume number, date, and pages of journal articles. Deciding on a note classification system that works reliably will save you time later on; it is extremely frustrating to fail to remember which source had the perfect table or inspiring quote. I use a system where each source has a simple code; each entry, note card, or photocopied page has a designator. This simply means a number or letter at the top, indicating a specific source, so all the vital bibliographical information is listed only once on a master file with one designator per entry. Another idea is to bookmark useful web sites on your computer.

3. *Develop a research vocabulary.* In the social sciences, as in any other field of endeavor, library reference works rely on vocabularies that convey large amounts of information in relatively little space. Thousands of books, journal articles, professional papers, dissertations, reviews, and other research reports are created each year, and keeping track of these materials poses formidable problems. Understanding even the nature of these sources can be formidable for the budding researcher. Many undergraduates fail to discern the difference between journals, publications with scholarly articles recounting the latest research, and magazines, resources intended for the general public that are not objective sources of information. Finding your way through the variety of written materials requires learning not just one but several methods of arranging information because research guides do not employ a standard vocabulary or format. Some are compiled by people, some by computers; depending on who or what has done the work, the information available will be more or less cryptic or timely. The description of the bibliographic guides that follows will acquaint you with some of the language of the library, but be prepared to spend some time getting to know how different library materials and computer files are arranged.

4. *Ask for help when you need it.* Do not hesitate to ask a librarian for assistance. Librarians are familiar with reference works, abstracts and indexes, computer databases, and other resources in

their collections and off campus. Many librarians have told me that students either neglect to consult them or wait too late to do so. These professionals will be able to more swiftly match your topic to the appropriate sources so that you can make the best use of your research time and maintain that necessary part-time job.

Although there are broad similarities among libraries, not all libraries are alike. These occasionally intimidating places differ in how materials are cataloged, where materials are stored, how they are obtained (e.g., open vs closed stacks), how and in what form the materials are kept (e.g., microfilm vs. bound volumes of journals), and in the library procedures for accessing information in electronic formats Libraries also differ greatly in their collections. A public library located in a small town may have a collection devoted chiefly to fiction and do-it-yourself books, with very little social science material, whereas a large university library system may have such an extensive social science collection that it must be housed in a separate building Whatever sort of library is available to you, attempt to find basic research materials locally first, to help you consider paper topics and approaches as early as possible. Often students consult highly specialized, or at the other extreme, unreliable sources on the Internet without first examining several approachable journal articles readily available in their local institution.

Just as library facilities differ from place to place, the type of research you may be asked to do will change as you progress through your academic career, from introductory classes to advanced degrees. Certainly not all research is done in a large library. In high school, for example, you may have used a bibliographic index entitled the *Readers' Guide to Periodical Literature* The range of topics covered and the materials indexed were both broad and general. The *Readers' Guide*, however, will not provide nearly enough information on sources for a paper written for a college social science course. For that, you need to use other specialized guides compiled primarily for scholarly research in the social sciences. Do not worry if you find complicated journal articles appropriate mainly for academic professionals;

you will eventually identify approachable materials at your current level of scholarship.

LIBRARIES, COMPUTERS, AND THE INTERNET

Libraries and computers are involved in a symbiotic relationship. As repositories of vast quantities of detailed, structured information, libraries are constantly changing and expanding. Computers, because of their ability to store large quantities of information and to edit, update, and retrieve this information quickly and easily, are well suited to manipulating this information In short, computers have changed the way libraries are organized, allowing for new and unprecedented ways of handling both printed and electronic information.

Virtually every aspect of information management in libraries has been touched by computer technology. Many important indexes and abstracts—in addition to data sources, such as the U.S. Census and the full text of journals—are now available as databases, either interactively online or in CD-ROM format. Computer technology allows you to cover vast quantities of citations in seconds, to tailor your search in a variety of ways not possible in print formats, and to obtain the most recent information. A statement about availability of each item in the collection is often integrated into the library's catalog. In addition, the online catalog can be searched more effectively than a simple alphabetical card catalog. For example, my library's catalog can be searched for "items nearby on shelf." Through the use of computer networks, such as the Internet, the collections of libraries, government documents, international organizations, and other sources not locally available can also be searched. It is often possible to download data or text from a computer database so that material can be integrated into your research paper using personal word processing software. This capability means that undergraduates can do more in-depth social science research than their predecessors because data collection is now so much easier.

The Internet is nothing but a set of computer protocols (capabilities or procedures) linking large and small computer networks. The three basic capabilities of the Internet are electronic mail (e-mail), file transfer, and remote login. *E-mail* provides rapid communication among researchers, teachers, and students, either individually or in shared group discussions often called "listservs," "mailing lists," or "Usenet newsgroups." Information about research in progress on your topic may be available in this form. Students in my classes have even contacted well-known researchers via e-mail about questions they may have about their work.

File-transfer protocol (FTP) allows you to download files from one computer to another. An institution or individual researcher chooses which files are made available. Programs, data sets, and text relevant to your topic might be transferred using FTP. *Telnet,* the ability to log in from your computer to a computer at another Internet institution anywhere in the world, is a major gateway for access to information about research. For example, your librarian can tell you how to telnet to the online catalog of the Library of Congress or to social and economic data generated by the U.S government.

Increasing numbers of electronic journals, publishing research results more rapidly than print journals, are available using telnet. Software programs enhancing Internet protocols continue to proliferate, with each new program offering more to the researcher. The World Wide Web (WWW), for example, makes it possible to send graphics, audio, and video over the Internet. In addition, the web provides hypertext links between documents. Selecting a linked word or picture in one document will instantly connect you to a related document, allowing you to creatively explore new ideas that spring from initial ones, rather like the act of writing itself described in Chapter 1.

The widespread incorporation of computer technology into research has introduced both benefits and liabilities to how library research is done. On the one hand, computers have expanded the scope of materials that can be searched and the precision with which they can be retrieved, accomplishing both tasks with remarkable speed. On the other hand, the sheer volume of material available through computer searching can easily overwhelm even experienced researchers, let alone stressed out undergraduates; moreover, accessing useful information requires basic skills, instruction, and documentation regarding how these systems work. Search software and protocols vary across databases and between libraries, and new technologies evolve rapidly. For example, it is essential to understand the utility of diverse search engines; the types used for general information are not often helpful for research at any academic level. You should consult your instructor or librarian for the best engine for the assignment in question. It should also be stressed that evaluating Internet sources is often difficult at first, for there are many unreliable, let alone not scholarly sources available One way to avoid this problem initially is to consult web site editions of prominent journals or reports from institutions that you see cited in textbooks or "hard cover" scholarly publications. Universities are also providing assistance to students on evaluating Internet materials. My library and writing center has links to organizations that have advice on evaluating sites, so the cure to Internet research woes may be found in the medium itself.

Despite the lack of standardization, there are two general elements of computer searching with which you should become familiar: learning the *basic characteristics of search software* and understanding how to determine the *scope and structure of a specific database.* All computer search software operates on the basis of character strings If a database uses a thesaurus of words and phrases to collate related material, this set of words and phrases is often the most efficient method of searching Before a search, for example, you might consult the printed or online versions of the *Thesaurus of Psychological Index Terms,* published by the American Psychological Association, or the *Thesaurus of Sociological Indexing Terms,* published by Sociological Abstracts Inc In these sources you will find terms such as "repression," which have specific meanings in each social science and lead to contrasting types of studies. These thesauri also list broader, narrower, or related terms useful in your search.

One of the most significant advances in indexing resulting from computer technology is the ability to provide "keyword" access to information. *Keywords* are significant words, defining your topic, that the computer searches within specified *fields* of text, such as in the titles or the abstracts of journal citations. For example, your keywords for an economics research paper might be "minority" and "business." Once you have identified a set of appropriate keywords, you can tailor your search in two ways: by specifying the relationship between keywords using logical operators, and by limiting the search to specific dates or fields. Three *logical operators* are commonly used to define the relationship between two (or more) search terms. "OR" retrieves all materials containing *any* (either one or both) of the search terms, thereby broadening a computer search. For example, I conducted a search of EconLit for the keyword "minority" and retrieved 398 bibliographic items. A search for the paired keywords "minority OR ethnic," however, retrieved 793 items.

By contrast, the logical operators "AND" and "NOT" narrow a search. To extend the previous example, a search for "minority NOT women" reduced the number of items found from 398 to 374. It is often more efficient, however, to focus the search using the operator "AND", retrieving only those entries that include two or more related keywords for your paper topic. To illustrate, the search statement "minority AND business" would produce materials that include both of these keywords, yielding 119 items in my search. There are also newer "Boolean" or logical operators, so you must always be open to exploring more powerful ways to search. For example, some systems use a symbol after a base word to expand the search; thus, I can add an asterisk after the key part of a word like aggression = aggress*, which will turn up citations including "aggressive," "aggressively," and so on, as well as "aggression."

In addition to the use of logical operators, computer searches can often be limited to specific fields (e.g., titles) or specific years of publication. In my revised search, I specified "minority AND business and PY > 1990" to retrieve 62 citations published after 1990 in which the two keywords "minority" and "business" appeared. In some systems, adjacency of keywords can be indicated, preassigned subject headings are available, or other features are provided to improve searching efficiency. Exactly what you will be able to do in a search depends on the scope and structure of the particular database in which you are working. For bibliographic databases that have a print counterpart (e.g., *Sociological Abstracts, Social Sciences Citation Index*), you can acquaint yourself with their organization by studying their printed versions, usually available in the reference section of major academic libraries. This is why I have included a discussion of printed bibliographic materials in subsequent sections of this chapter. For other databases, you will have to rely on documentation supplied by software vendors or on help sheets written by librarians at your institution.

The basic characteristics of search software described in this section are evident in the WWW "search engines" developed for identifying relevant documents, data, electronic journals, guides, or listservs and newsgroups on the Internet. Some search engines display reliable links in browseable subject groupings, such as social sciences, economics, and psychology. Some offer keyword indexing based on comprehensive automated surveys of all registered Internet sites. Meta-indexes permitting searches across search engines also exist, and again you need to learn which ones are best for serious study in the social sciences. Given the fast-changing, competitive technology of the Internet, newer and better indexes will evolve almost monthly. Your reference librarian is the best source for up-to-date advice on which search engines to use and their current WWW addresses (called URLs, uniform resource locators).

GETTING STARTED: VOCABULARY AND CONCEPTS

Just as you cannot know exactly what you will say in a paper until you begin to write (and not even then, because you will keep revising what you write), you cannot expect to know what library or Internet materials will be best suited to your needs until you begin searching for them. A good place to start is with *specialized encyclopedias and dictionaries*. Unlike general reference works such as *Webster's Collegiate Dictionary* or the *Encyclopaedia Britannica*, these volumes address particular topics within a discipline and provide more than brief definitions of social science concepts. Specialized dictionaries and encyclopedias offer background discussions of the major issues and problems identified with a topic, using the language of scholars who write about these issues. These resources place your potential paper in a context, so you can determine how sound your idea may be and how it fits in with research in the discipline. Developing a vocabulary relevant to your interests will assist you at a later point in your library search, such as when you look for subject headings or keywords in the library catalog.

Specialized encyclopedias can also be used directly in your paper when you incorporate them into your review, found at the beginning of most social science papers, of major research findings. The entries in these works are prepared by experts who, because of space limitations, usually confine their review to significant, well-documented research findings in their field. What you read in these reference works is therefore likely to provide concise, basic information.

Finally, entries in these dictionaries and encyclopedias are often followed by selective bibliographies that include many references not directly discussed by the authors of the cited articles. You can use these bibliographies to initiate your library research because they will probably include significant research conducted on a topic before the entry was written. Because these volumes are not revised frequently, however, you should turn to other sources for brief overviews of more contemporary research. Recently published textbooks often include such up-to-date bibliographies, as do periodic reviews of the literature, such as the *Annual Review of Anthropology,* the *Annual Review of Psychology,* and the *Annual Review of Sociology.*

Each discipline has at least one major dictionary and encyclopedia that can help you start your library research, and often you will find specialized volumes covering subfields that bridge disciplinary boundaries (e.g., *The Encyclopedia of Aging*). Depending on the discipline in which you are working, you might consider consulting the following dictionaries and encyclopedias (these are the latest editions).

Dictionaries

Dictionary of Concepts in Cultural Anthropology (1991)

Dictionary of Concepts in Physical Anthropology (1991)

The MIT Dictionary of Modern Economics (1992)

The Dictionary of Twentieth Century World Politics (1993)

The HarperCollins Dictionary of American Government and Politics (1992)

The International Dictionary of Psychology (1989)

The Blackwell Dictionary of Sociology (1995)

Dictionary of Statistics and Methodology: A Nontechnical Guide for the Social Sciences (1993)

Encyclopedias

The Social Sciences Encyclopedia, second ed. (1996)

Companion Encyclopedia of Anthropology (1994)

Encyclopedia of World Cultures (1991–)

The McGraw-Hill Encyclopedia of Economics (1994)

The Oxford Companion to Politics of the World (1993)

Encyclopedia of Psychology, second ed. (1994)

Encyclopedia of Sociology (1992)

INDEXES AND ABSTRACTS

Indexes and abstracts are probably the most important bibliographic tools of the social scientist. Like dictionaries and encyclopedias, these reference works are specialized guides to the myriad topics of interest to social scientists. However, unlike dictionaries, these useful tools go beyond a brief introduction to a social process or institution; they help you identify scholarly research that has been conducted on some topic in which you are interested. Indexes and abstracts are also likely to be compiled frequently, and are now available on the Internet, so that they contain recently published research. Many printed indexes and abstracts are generated from computer databases that are updated regularly. A number of electronic indexes are linked directly to computer files of full texts of the articles indexed. Your library may make it possible for you to print out articles immediately, to send them to yourself via e-mail, or to order them (usually for a fee) from a document delivery company providing same day or next-day fax service. Sometimes online articles may have a different form than the journal paper copy, but that is mainly a concern for upper-level researchers.

Even if you have never conducted research in the social sciences, you have probably used an index at some time. Your high school or public library no doubt had copies of the *Readers' Guide to Periodical Literature.* Arranged alphabetically by subject and author, the *Readers' Guide* indexes a number of magazines that are of broad public interest, such as *Psychology Today, The New Republic,* and *Scientific American.* These magazines seldom report primary research and, consequently, are not particularly helpful in writing most college-level papers. The research you need will be found in indexes for scholarly journals in different academic fields. The two indexes most frequently used by social scientists are *Social Sciences Index* and *Social Sciences Citation Index.*

A note on printed materials versus computer searches: Although many of the indexes and abstracts discussed in the following section are available through searches of online databases, I have included information on how to conduct a bibliographic search using the printed versions of these materials. Becoming familiar with the printed versions of *Social Sciences Index* or *Social Sciences Citation Index,* for example, will improve your understanding of their computerized counterparts, thereby increasing your chances of generating a useful set of references using a computer search. There is also a chance that you may find yourself working in a library, or perhaps on your PC at home, where computerized searches are either too difficult or too costly to arrange. In these cases, you can always fall back on the printed versions of abstracts and indexes available at your library.

Social Sciences Index

The *Social Sciences Index* is the simplest guide to social science journal literature because it is limited to about 350 important English-language journals. It is arranged much like the *Readers' Guide,* by subject and author, is published four times a year, and cumulated into annual volumes. *Social Sciences Index* is also available in a number of electronic forms—as an online or CD-ROM database, or as an enhancement to computerized library catalogs.

For the purpose of illustration, assume that you have decided to write a research paper on the general topic of retirement communities. You may wonder, for example, why some people choose to leave their homes and move to age-segregated communities in Florida or Arizona on retirement, or what retirees spend their time doing in these communities, or whether these migrants are happier after they relocate. You probably will not be able to address all of these questions in your paper, but you have narrowed your topic sufficiently to start for the library. After beginning your library search by examining a specialized encyclopedia, dictionary, or annual review, you look for any entries in *Social Sciences Index* under the heading "Retirement communities" or a related phrase (see Figure 2.1). For Internet searches, the specific phrase you choose can save you time by identifying the best sources early on.

In this issue of the index, there are three listings under the heading of "Retirement communities," the third of which is a study of widows in retirement communities. The listing gives the authors' names (L. K. Hong and R. W. Duff), the journal in which it appears (*Gerontologist*), and the volume number (34), page numbers (347–352), and date of publication (June 1994) of the article.

Retiree tax, benefits bills move forward in House. D. Masci. *Congr Q Wkly Rep* v52 p2891 O 8 '94
Retirement communities
    See also
       Life care communities
Paradise lost: widowhood in a Florida retirement community. D. K. van den Hoonaard. bibl *J Aging Stud* v8 p121–32 Summ '94
Retiring where the mariachis play: in Mexico, a retired couple can live luxuriously on $1,500 a month. P. Kephart. *Am Demogr* v16 p20–1 N '94
Widows in retirement communities: the social context of subjective well-being. L. K. Hong and R. W. Duff. bibl *Gerontologist* v34 p347–52 Je '94
Retirement income
    See also
       Pensions
The effect of job mobility on pension wealth. S. A. Mehdizadeh and R. A. Luzadis. bibl *Gerontologist* v34 p173–9 Ap '94
Police pension and retirement system· a deferred option plan. T. G. Carlton. *FBI Law Enforc Bull* v63 p23–5 Ap '94
Portability of pension benefits among jobs. A. C. Foster. *Mon Labor Rev* v117 p45–50 Jl '94
Retirement benefits in the 1990s [review article] M. Bucci. *Mon Labor Rev* v117 p55–6 Jl '94
Sources of growth and cyclical stability for Nevada counties: transfer payments and property income. G. W. Smith and T. R. Harris. *Soc Sci J* v30 no4 p301–21 '93
Status maintenance and change during old age. F. C. Pampel and M. Hardy. bibl *Soc Forces* v73 p289–314 S '94
Working-class women and retirement. K. Perkins. bibl *J Gerontol Soc Work* v20 no3–4 p129–46 '93
Retirement pensions *See* Pensions
Retouching (Photography) *See* Photography—Retouching
Retributive damages *See* Punitive damages
Retributive theory of justice *See* Punishment
Retrieval of information *See* Information systems
Retroactive inhibition *See* Inhibition (Psychology)
Retroactive judicial decisions *See* Retroactive laws and decisions

■ *Figure* 2.1

From *Social Sciences Index.*

An entry such as this is fairly unambiguous because the location of the article (*Gerontologist*) is spelled out completely. Usually journal titles are abbreviated (e.g., *Am Stat, Dev Psychol, J Reg Sci, QJ Econ*), and you must look in the front of the index for a key to deciphering these cryptic references. If the title of the article looks promising, all you need to do is determine whether your library subscribes to the journal you need. If your library does not have the journal, you can probably obtain a copy through interlibrary loan. For students at most universities, journal articles can now be read online or printed out for a nominal fee.

The *Social Sciences Index* will also often refer you to additional topic headings. In our example, there is a note to "*See also* Life care communities." *See also* means that research of *related* interest appears under the alternative heading or headings in the index. *See* means that the index uses a master or preferred heading other than the one you have consulted to identify research on this topic. For example, under the heading "Retributive theory of justice" you will find "*See* Punishment." In the future, you need only look under "Punishment" in the index to find any work that might have been done on retributive justice.

Social Sciences Citation Index (SSCI)

The *Social Sciences Citation Index* (*SSCI*) is a good deal more complicated than the *Social Sciences Index,* but it is well worth your time to learn to use it. Because it is computer generated, the *SSCI* indexes more journals than most other reference works, and it does so fairly quickly, making it a good print source for identifying relatively recent research. But because it has been generated by a machine, using the *SSCI* requires that you develop a slightly different approach to locate research materials (*Current Contents: Social and Behavioral Sciences,* a weekly publication containing the tables of contents of several major journals, is published between printings of the *SSCI,* providing a guide to the more recent research.) As expectations of your research expertise increase, you will need to find, consult, and use the most professional sources available.

The *SSCI* is divided into three parts: the "Permuterm Index," a listing of entries by subject keywords; the "Source Index," a listing of articles arranged by author; and the "Citation Index," a listing of authors cited in footnotes of published work. Each of these is bound as a separate section of the *SSCI.* Using the *SSCI* involves a series of steps leading from one index to another

The Permuterm Index is the appropriate starting place if you are searching for material on a specific topic. This part of the index categorizes articles according to pairs of significant words appearing in the *titles*. Because no human judgment intervenes to bring articles on a topic together under broad subject headings, you will spend some time sifting out articles only to find, when you locate them, that you cannot use them in your paper. This is not much of a problem in our example of retirement communities, however, because both words are likely to be used in the titles of relevant journal articles. In the excerpt shown in Figure 2.2, the primary term *Retirement* is followed by more than 75 words that have been paired with it in titles Looking down the column headed "Retirement," we locate the word *Communities* and find that there are two articles in which both of these words appear. The symbols appearing *after* the authors' names provide additional information: "@" means that this issue of *SSCI* lists more than one article by this author on this topic; "+" indicates that the article is, in fact, a book review. The symbol "?" *before* an author's name indicates its first appearance under the primary search term; every other occurrence of this author's name under this primary term will lead you to the same article and, thus, can be ignored.

Looking down the list of other words appearing under the primary term *Retirement,* you can see that searching for useful references is not always so straightforward. For example, is relevant information contained in the article by Hargrave that pairs *Retirement* with *Property,* or the article by Newcomer that pairs *Retirement* with the term *Community?* Your search may be further complicated by a range of related, but independent topics appearing nearby in the index. Above the term *Retirement* are listed *Retire, Retired, Retired-Worker,* and *Retirees.* Any or all of these listings may contain potentially helpful materials for your paper; the number of leads you pursue is constrained by the time you have to devote to library research. But no matter how little time you may have to spend on the project, begin by considering all of the possible ways your topic might be listed.

Once you have located an entry that seems promising, how do you find out more about it? The next step is to locate the author's name in the Source Index. Suppose you are interested in the article

RETINOPATHY
CHLORPROMA ▸MITCHELL
AC

RETIRE
ABROAD   ·-▸MARTIN J
FIRED ····▸MAYES RT
GETS ····   "
IF ·······MARTIN J
JIM ·····-MAYES RT
MARCH-APRIL.
"
PG ·······   "
RATHER ··-MARTIN J
READERS · ·MAYES RT
REPLY ···   "
TODAY ···▸KUMN SE
WAITING ··MAYES RT
YOUD ····-MARTIN J

RETIRED
EMPLOYEES▸MAKOFSKY   A
PUBLIC ···   "
UNION ····   "

RETIRED . . . THE
CAREER -HEINBUCH SE +
GUIDE ····   "   +
NEVER–WANT.
"   +
$OON-TO-BE.
"   +

RETIRED-WORKER
BENEFIT -▸BONDAR J
COMPUTE -   "

RETIREES
BOREDOM ▸WEINSTEI.L
GROUP ····   "
LIFE ····   "
PURPOSE -   "
VOLUNTEERI.
"

RETIREMENT
········▸FERGUS C
········▸HERBST R
········▸PAGAC KH
ACCOUNTS ▸HARGRAVE   L
AGE   ·····▸PINQUART   M
ANXIETY ▸MACEWEN   KE
ASSISTED-L.   ▸NEWCOMER
R
BEHAVIOR ▸LEGRAND   TK
BENEFICIAR.   ▸BIXBY   AK
BENEFITS ·   "
BRAZIL ·-LEGRAND TK
CARE   -NEWCOMER   R
CHANGES -▸RUHM CJ.
CHINA ····-▸DAVIS D +
CITY ·····▸LAWS G
CLOSE ···▸KUEHLWEI.M
········-PINQUART M
COLLEGE -▸SPIERS J
COMMUNITIES ▸EDUC
GERON +
········-LAWS G
COMMUNITY   HARGRAVE   L
·   -NEWCOMER   R
CONDITIONS▸DORFMAN   LT
CONTINUING   NEWCOMER
R
COSTS ···SPIERS J
COVER · -▸J TAXATION ■
DETERMINAN.   LEGRAND TK
DEVELOPMEN. ▸CARLSSON
B
DISCRIMINA.   ▸ARBER S +
DISSAVING KUEHLWEI.M
DONT ····-SPIERS J
EARLY ···-CARLSSON B
········-▸HERZ DE

EFFICIENCY ▸BLANCHET   D
EGG ·   -▸KRUTHOFF.R +
EMPLOYEESJ   TAXATION   ■
EQUITY ·--BLANCHET D
FISCAL ···-BIXBY AK
FUNCTIONS BLANCHET D
GERMAN ·-·PINQUART M
GONE ····-▸FRANKE AH
HAD ·   -J TAXATION ■
HEALTH ··-▸COSTA DL
········-DORFMAN LT
HISTORY ··-KUEHLWEI.M
IDENTITIES LAWS G
INCOME · -COSTA DL
INDIVIDUAL HARGRAVE L
INSURANCE BLANCHET D
INTERESTS HARGRAVE L
LANDSCAPE LAWS G
LEAVE ·   -▸DICESARE CB
LONGITUDIN.   KUEHLWEI.M
MANDATORY   FRANKE   AH
MEN ·····-RUHM CJ
MENS ····-LEGRAND TK
MYTH ·····▸BARTH J +
NEST ·   -KRUTHOFF.R +
NEW ·····   +
········-PINQUART M
NURSES -▸MOORE K
NURSING NEWCOMER   R
OLDER · -PINQUART M
········-RUHM CJ
PART-TIME J TAXATION ■
PATTERNS -RUHM CJ
PENSIONS -ARBER S +
········-▸COSTA DL
PERCEIVED DORFMAN LT
PERSONS · ·PINQUART M
PLAN ·   -J TAXATION ■
PLANNING -▸HADJIAN A
POSSIBILITY   PINQUART   M
PRE-RETIRE.   BLANCHET   D
PREDICTING MACEWEN   KE
PREGNANCY   DICESARE   CB
PREPARATION MOORE   K
PROPERTY HARGRAVE L
PUBLIC-EMP.   BIXBY   AK
QUALITY-OF.   DORFMAN LT
RAIN ·   -▸SPIERS J
REPRESENTA.   LAWS G
RESIDENTS NEWCOMER   R
REVOLUTION.   DAVIS D +
SCHEME · -CARLSSON B
SECULAR -RUHM CJ
STATES · · -PINQUART M
SUN ·   -LAWS G
SURVEY · -KUEHLWEI.M
SWEDISH -CARLSSON B
SYSTEMS -BIXBY AK
········-BLANCHET D
TIME ·   -▸CARROLL   E +
·   ·   -▸HERAULT   B +
UNEMPLOYED PINQUART M
UNIT ·   -NEWCOMER   R
UNIVERSITY.   EDUC GERON
N +
USE ·   -NEWCOMER   R
WOMEN · -▸SLEVIN KF
WORK ····-HERZ DE
········-RUHM CJ
YEAR ····-BIXBY AK
2ND ·····-HADJIAN A

RETRAINING
ON-THE-JOB▸NORDHAUS.AM

■ *Figure 2.2*

From *SSCI Permuterm Index*, May to August 1995

by G. Laws listed under the paired words *Retirement* and *Communities*. The Source Index listing for G. Laws identifies four articles, two of which are book reviews (see Figure 2.3). The third listing is the one you were searching for, as it contains the keywords *retirement* and *communities:* "Embodiment and Emplacement—Identities, Representation and Landscape in Sun City Retirement Communities." In addition to the title of the article, the citation includes where it was published (*Int J Aging,* an abbreviation of a journal entitled *International Journal of Aging and Human Development*) the volume and number of the journal (Volume 40, Number 4), the page numbers (pages 253–280), and the year of publication (1995). The small print below this information about the article gives G. Laws's affiliation, followed by the references cited in the article. These references are listed by author's name, year and place of publication, and page number.

You might end your search for journal articles here, armed with a list of references gathered from the Source Index that leads you to the library journal collection. In the course of your research, however, you might find that articles written by some scholars are particularly useful and that you would like to identify other researchers who have found these articles helpful in their own work. You can do this by exploring the third part of the *SSCI*. The Citation Index lists all of the works written by a particular author that have been cited by other scholars in journals indexed in that issue of *SSCI*. If this article is a major piece of research, the number of citations is a vital clue to identifying its importance for your study. If you want to know who has cited Laws's previous work, you would look for "Laws G" in the Citation Index and find several entries (see Figure 2.4). Consider the following entry:

94 POLIT GEOGR 13 7
HARPER S PROG H GEOG 19 199 95 R

The information in the first line of the entry refers to an article written by Laws in 1994, appearing in *Political Geography,* Volume 13, page 7. This article was cited by S. Harper in *Progress in Human Geography,* Volume 19, page 199 in 1995. A letter following the

LAWRY S
see HAZZARD ACHILD ABUSE   19   707   95

LAWS G
GEOGRAPHY AND SOCIAL-JUSTICE—SMITH, DM & BOOK
REVIEW
ANN AS AM G   85(2):390–392   95   RK691
PENN STATE UNIV, DEPT GEOG, UNIVERSITY PK, PA 16802, USA
FULL CIRCLE—GEOGRAPHIES OF WOMEN OVER THE
LIFE COURSE—KATZ, C, MONK, J & BOOK REVIEW
GROWTH CHAN 2 6(2) 330–333   95   RL582
PENN STATE UNIV, UNIVERSITY PK, PA 16802, USA
EMBODIMENT AND EMPLACEMENT—IDENTITIES
REPRESENTATION AND LANDSCAPE IN SUN CITY RETIREMENT
COMMUNITIES
INT J AGING   40(4):253–280   95 60R   RM868
PENN STATE UNIV, DEPT GEOG, 302 WALKER BLDG, UNIVERSITY PK,
PA 16802, USA

ACHENBAUM WA	78	OLD AGE NEW LAND AM		
BERGSMAN S	91	PHOENIX MAGAZINE AUG	9	939
BIRD J	93	MAPPING FUTURES LOCA	120	
CHUDACOFF H	89	OLD ARE YOU AGE CONS		
CLARK WAV	86	HUMAN MIGRATION		
COLE T	92	JOURNEY LIFE CULTURA		
COLE TR	93	VOICES VISIONS AGING		
CONNOR K	92	AGING AM ISSUES FACI		
DANIELS S	89	NEW MODELS GEOGRAPHY	2	196
DAVIES M	90	CITY QUARTZ EXCAVATI		34
DIAMOND E	93	NEW CHOICES RETIREME		147
DOWD J	86	LATER LIFE SOCIAL PS		136
DUNN P	93	MAPPING FUTURES LOCA	9	134
EMERSON RW	1862	ATLANTIC MONTHLY		3719
FEATHERSTONE M	90	BODY SOCIAL PROCESS		265
"	92	MODERNITY IDENTITY		
FINDLAY J	92	MAGIC LANDS W CITYSC		
FITZGERALD F	86	CITIES HILL		28
FLANAGAN B	92	NEW CHOICES RETIREME		
FOUCAULT M	77	LANGUAGE COUNTER MEM9	80	
"		POWER KNOWLEDGE		
FOUCAULT M	86	DIACRITICS 16	22	
FRIEDAN B	63	FEMININE MYSTIQUE		
GALLAGHER W	93	ATLANTIC 271	52	
GARREAU J	91	EDGE CITY LIFE NEW F		134
GRATTON B	93	VOICES VISIONS AGING		
HABER C	83	83		
HABERMAS J	85	HABERMAS IDENTITY		
HARAWAY D	90	FEMINISM POSTMODERN		196
HARVEY D	89	CONDITION POSTMODERN		
HASSAN I	85	THEORY CULTURE SOC	2	???
HEPWORTH M	82	SURVIVING MIDDLE AGE		???
HOFFMANNAXTHELM D	92	MODERNITY IDENTITY		3
HOUSEMAN W	92	NEW CHOICES RETIREME	32	201
JACKSON P	93	MAPPING FUTURES LOCA		
JACOBS J	61	DEATH LIFE GREAT AM		160
KASTENBAUM R	93	VOICES VISIONS AGING		
KRISTEVA J	82	POWERS HORROR		
LASH S	92	MODERNITY IDENTITY		
LAWS G	93	ANN ASSOC AM GEOGR	83	672
LEY D	81	BEHAVIORAL PROBLEMS		209
LUKIN S	91	LANDSCAPES POWER DET		
MEINIG D	79	INTERPRETATION ORDIN		
MOODY H	93	VOICES VISIONS AGING		R 15
PANITT M	93	NEW CHOICES RETIREME		12
PUTMAN T	93	MAPPING FUTURES LOCA		130
RICH A	86	BLOOD BREAD POETRY		
ROWLES GD	81	GERONTOLOGIST	21	304
SELIGSON M	93	NEW CHOICES RETIREME		44
SHAPIRO M	92	READING POSTMODERN P		
SOJA E	89	POSTMODERN GEOGRAPHI		
SORKIN M	92	VARIATIONS THEME PAR		
STALLYBRASS P	86	POLITICS POETICS TRA		
STEARNS PN	80	J FAMILY HIST 5	44	
WALBY S	90	THEORIZING PATRIARCH		
WALLACE S	92	SENIOR MOVEMENT REFE		
WARD A	93	ARCHITECTURE COMPORT	9	39
WEISS M	89	CLUSTERING AM		
YOUNG IM	90	JUSTICE POLITICS DIF		

SOCIAL-JUSTICE AND URBAN-POLITICS—AN INTRODUCTION
URBAN GEOGR 15(7):603–611   94   24R   X658
PENN STATE UNIV, DEPT GEOG UNIVERSITY PK, PA 16802, USA

CASTELLS M	78	CITY CLASS POWER		
COLLINS PH	86	SOC PROBL 33	S 14	
DEAR M	81	URBANIZATION URBAN P		
GUINIER L	94	TYRANNY MAJORITY FUN		
HARDING S	91	WHOSE SCI WHOSE KNOW		
HARVEY D	73	SOCIAL JUSTICE CITY		
"	92	INT J URBAN REGIONAL	16	580
JAMISON A	94	SEEDS SIXTIES		
KATZNELSON I	81	CITY TRENCHES		
KOBAYASHI A	94	PROF GEOGR 46	73	
LARANA E	94	NEW SOCIAL MOVEMENTS		
LASLETT P	92	JUSTICE AGE GROUPS G		
LORDE A	84	SISTER OUTSIDER		
LOSEKE D	92	BATTERED WOMAN SHELT		
OLIVER M	90	POLITICS DISABLEMENT		
PRATT H	93	GRAY AGENDAS INTERES		
PULIDO L	94	ENVIRON PLANN A	26	925
RAWLS J	71	THEORY JUSTICE		
SCOTT A	90	IDEALOGY NEW SOCIAL		
SMITH D	94	GEOGRAPHY SOCIAL JUS		
SMITH DM	77	HUMAN GEOGRAPHY WELF		
TABB W	78	MARXISM METROPOLIS		
TRACEY LH	50	MY HEART SANG STORY		
YOUNG IM	90	JUSTICE POLITICS DIF		
see HARPER S		PROG H GEOG	19 199	95

LAWS J
see IOANNIDI C   J FORECAST   14   51   95

LAWS K
MCCARTHY RA—ATTRIBUTES, CATEGORIES, AND MODALITIES—EVIDENCE FOR DIS-
SOCIATION IN CASES OF SEMANTIC CATEGORY IMPAIRMENT & MEETING ABSTRACT

■ Figure 2.3

From SSCI Source Index, May to August 1995.

```
91 ADV BEHAV RES THER       13   13
  LEITENBE H    PSYCHOL B    117  469   95   R
  LOOMAN J      CAN J BEH S   27  321   95
LAWS G
  ''IN PRESS J AGING STU
  88 T I BRIT GEOGR          13   433
  89 POWER GEOGRAPHY        P238
  92 CONT RURAL SYSTEMS T
  HARPER S      PROG H GEOG   19  199   95   R
  93 ANN ASSOC AM GEOGR      83  672
  HARPER S      PROG H GEOG   19  199   95   R
  LAWS G  INT J AGING        40  253   95
  94 ENVIRON PLANN A         26 1787
  94 POLIT GEOGR             13   7
  HARPER S      PROG H GEOG   19  199   95   R
  94 POLITICAL GEOGRAPHY     13   7
  ENGLAND K     URBAN GEOGR   15  628   94
  95 GERONTOLOGIST           35  112
  95 INT J AGING HUM DEV    P45
  HARPER S      PROG H GEOG   19  199   95   R
LAWS JL
  80 LIFE-SPAN DEV BEHAV      3  207
  VONSYDOW K  ARCH SEX BE     24  271   95
LAWS JV
  89 ERGONOMICS              32 1303
  SHIFFER MJ    ENVIR PL B    22  359   95
```

■ *Figure* 2.4

From *SSCI Citation Index*, May to August 1995

entry denotes a type of source item other than an article or a report. The "R" following the listing indicates that Harper's item is a review; other letters correspond to chronologies, editorials, and technical notes. After glancing through the citation index, you might notice that Harper has referred to Laws's work several times; therefore, you may decide to quickly explore Harper's work to see whether it is relevant to your study To find out more about Harper's article, you would return to the Source Index section of the *SSCI* for the appropriate year (1995) and look at the listings for S. Harper. Researching entries in the Citation Index reveals an interrelated network of references, some of which you might have missed in your original examination of the Permuterm Index.

    SSCI is available both online and in CD-ROM versions.

Dissertation Abstracts International (DAI)

Abstracts differ from indexes, in that they provide more information. As their name implies, abstracts give you a summary of an article, as well as its title and citation. Abstracts allow you to judge, with some confidence, which articles will be useful, another way to speed and refine your study.

    Doctoral dissertations, while at times too specialized for undergraduates, nonetheless are useful in identifying the latest research before it has been formally published. The abstracts of doctoral dissertations are published 12 times each year in two sets of *Dissertation Abstracts International (DAI)*. Social sciences and humanities dissertations appear in issues marked "A," natural science and psychology dissertations in issues marked "B." Entries in *DAI* are arranged in broad categories and are also indexed by keywords from the titles of the dissertations. A wide variety of research may be presented in a single category label, but dissertation title and area of specialization will help you identify potentially helpful research.

Under the heading "Retirement communities," excerpted from the index for *DAI* and shown in Figure 2.5, is listed a thesis on continuing care retirement communities. The number that follows the title indicates that the thesis is abstracted on page 3844 of part A of *DAI*. On that page, in addition to the abstract itself, the institution where the thesis was submitted, the date when it was published, and its length are given (see Figure 2.6). The chair of the student's thesis committee is often listed as well.

You should probably explore the other indexes and abstracts I have mentioned before settling down in front of *DAI*. Although they often provide an up-to-date review of the literature in a particular field, obtaining dissertations can be both costly and time consuming. Universities that contribute to *DAI* do not lend the original dissertation, relying instead on University Microfilms International to sell microfilm copies (or, at a premium price, paper reproductions) to li-

Morris, Barbara B., p.3715A

Retirement
Retirement style, postretirement work pattern, and retirement satisfaction of public school administrators. *Cooper, Daniel Frank, p.3642A*

Retirement communities
An analysis of the effect of admission and transfer policies on nursing care use patterns in continuing care retirement communities. *George, Eda Upham, p.3844A*

■ *Figure* 2.5

From *DAI*

An analysis of the effect of admission and transfer policies on nursing care use patterns in continuing care retirement communities. George, Eda Upham, Ph.D. *Brandeis University, The Florence Heller Graduate School for Advanced Studies in Social Welfare,* 1993. *161pp.* Adviser: Christine E. Bishop

Order Number DA9408862

The major thesis of this work is that management policies affect nursing home utilization at Continuing Care Retirement Communities (CCRCs). The research examines the relationships between nursing home utilization patterns and admission and transfer policies and resident and CCRC characteristics.

As organizations that do not rely on public funding for their residents' social and health needs, CCRCs provide a finance and delivery system with special factors that influence the use of nursing home care. Understanding how policies may affect the utilization of nursing care provides insight into the financing and delivery of long-term care services in general.

Using data from the 1989 National Continuing Care Data Base, the study includes analysis of resident, CCRC and management information as well as predictions of nursing home use by CCRC residents.

The research builds upon theoretical and practical research in CCRCs that has examined the relationships between nursing home utilization and characteristics of CCRCs. After a review of the literature, hypotheses are developed for examination and discussion.

The analyses indicate that CCRCs that deny admission to applicants with organic brain syndrome and use standardized transfer policies tend to have a higher proportion of their residents using nursing home care. In addition, the analyses of the patterns of use indicate that differences are observed according to the health guarantee, the age of the community, and the extent of use of assisted living services by residents.

■ *Figure 2.6*

From *DAI.*

braries and researchers. Most dissertations that have been purchased by libraries are now available through interlibrary loan, but in isolated cases you will have to purchase the copy directly from University Microfilms International. If you are working on a long-term project, such as writing a master's thesis, and after reading a particular abstract, you feel that the complete dissertation would be extremely helpful, it may be worth your time and expense to order it. Otherwise, you can expect much thesis research to appear in following years in other forms, as young scholars revise their work for publication in journals and books. *DAI* is available both online and in CD-ROM versions. The texts of the abstracts can be searched by keywords. If you attend a small college, there are dissertations and other sources in nearby large research universities; it may be worth a trip.

Abstracts and Indexes for Specific Disciplines

Specialized abstracts and indexes are available for each social science discipline. Anthropological research is abstracted in *Abstracts in Anthropology* and indexed in *Anthropological Literature*, psychological research is abstracted in *Psychological Abstracts*, sociological research is abstracted in *Sociological Abstracts*, and economic and political science research is indexed in the *PAIS International in Print*. (PAIS is an acronym for Public Affairs Information Service.) Although these bibliographical sources differ from one another in exactly how they are organized, they all rely on indexing by keywords or subject headings to guide the search. Only *Abstracts in Anthropology* is not available in computer format.

THE LIBRARY'S CATALOG

Research appearing in journals will probably constitute the bulk of references you use in any type of social science writing, but, in addition to these, you will want to explore other formats used to report research. It is certainly true that for those beginning to write social science papers some journals will be too arcane, both in their methodology and in readability. Sometimes books are a logical place to look, both to give needed background, and for example in political science, as a resource themselves. The memoirs written by Mikail Gorbachev are valuable primary resources for Russian studies. If you know an expert on your topic, you can go directly to the author's name to see whether your library has any books written by this scholar. Otherwise, your efforts are best spent searching for any materials housed in your library that pertain to your specific subject. To do this effectively, you need to know something about the subject headings used by libraries to bring together related books.

Most libraries use the Library of Congress subject headings. The first step, then, is to make sure that you search for your topic using the appropriate vocabulary. A convenient way to do this is to consult *Library of Congress Subject Headings*. (If your library uses the Dewey decimal system, however, consult *Sears List of Subject Headings*.) If you searched for materials pertaining to retirement and retirement communities in the Library of Congress listing, you would find the headings shown in Figure 2.7.

Any word or phrase appearing in boldface type (e.g., **Retirement communities**) is a heading that may be used in the catalog. Following this heading is the phrase "May Subd Geog," meaning that the heading may be subdivided by location. Indented below a heading and prefixed by either "BT" (for "broader topic") or "NT" (for "narrower topic") are other headings used in the catalog. (In this example, you are referred to the broader topics "Aged—Dwellings" and "Retirement, Places of," and the narrower topic "Life care communities.") A word or phrase preceded by "UF" (meaning "used for") is *not* used in the catalog; information on these topics (e.g., "Mandatory retirement") is found instead under the boldface heading that comes before these phrases ("Retirement, Mandatory").

The "RT" prefix stands for "related topic," providing a cross-reference of subject headings. For example, under "Retirement Mandatory," "Retirement age" is prefixed by "RT." Under the boldface heading "**Retirement age**," there is an "RT" reference to "Retirement, Mandatory." Words or phrases prefixed by a dash indicate a subheading of the major topic heading ("**Retirement, Mandatory**," "**—Law and legislation**"). Headings that appear in lightface type are not used in the catalog, but you are directed to see the proper heading, prefaced by the word "USE" (e.g., information on "Retirement pensions" is found under "Civil service—Pensions," "Old age pensions," and "Pensions").

Because "**Retirement communities**" is a recognized (boldface) heading in the Library of Congress list, you can use the heading to search the catalog. The scope note under the phrase points out the distinction between retirement communities and life care

UF   Mandatory retirement
RT   Retirement age
—**Law and legislation**   *(May Subd Geog)*
        BT   Labor laws and legislation
Retirement, Places of   *(May Subd Geog)*
UF   Places of retirement
NT   Retirement communities
Retirement accounts, Individual
USE   Individual retirement accounts
Retirement age   *(May Subd Geog)*
        [HD7105-HD7106]
UF   Age of retirement
Pension age
        BT   Age and employment
        RT   Retirement, Mandatory
Retirement benefits
USE   Postemployment benefits
Retirement communities   *(May Subd Geog)*
        Here are entered works on planned resi-
dential developments designed for the aged.
Works on planned residential developments
for the aged which also provide meal service,
medical care, etc. are entered under Life care
communities.
        BT   Aged—Dwellings
Retirement, Places of
        NT   Life care communities
        —**Activity programs**
            UF   Activity programs for retirement
                 communities
Retirement contributions as tax deductions
        USE   Income tax—Deductions—Retirement
                contributions
Retirement income   *(May Subd Geog)*
        BT   Income
        NT   Pensions
        —**Effect of inflation on**
        BT   Inflation (Finance)
Retirement pensions
        USE   Civil service—Pensions
                Old age pensions
                Pensions
Retirement test (Old age pensions)
        USE   Old age pensions—Retirement test

■ *Figure* 2.7

From *Library of Congress Subject Headings.*

communities. Of late, most libraries have alternative systems that identify keywords used in academic databases, the most common of which is "Words in the Title."

Many libraries have replaced their card catalogs or microformat catalogs with computer terminals directly connected to a database recording the holdings of the library. Because these documentation procedures vary from library to library, the formats for displaying information about library holdings are no longer uniform. An online search for materials on retirement communities at my college library displayed the entry in Figure 2.8.

The bibliographic information on the computer screen includes, in labeled fields, the author (Charles F. Longino), the title of the book (*Retirement Migration in America*), the publisher and date of publication (Vacation Publications, 1995), book length (185 pages), and the subject heading under which the book is classified (Retirees—United States—Statistics). A note indicates that there is a useful bibliography of references, a sign that the book is a serious study. The bottom line on the screen indicates the number of copies (1), the location of the book in the college library system (Clapp Library, in the Reference Section), the library call number (HQ1063.2.U6 L65 1995), and the loan status of the book.

CALL #	HQ1063.2.U6 L65 1995.
LOCATIONS	Clapp Ref
AUTHOR	Longino, Charles F., 1938-
TITLE	Retirement migration in America / Charles F. Longino,
Jr.;	
	edited by R. Alan Fox.
IMPRINT	Houston : Vacation Publications, c1995.
DESCRIPT.	185 p. : maps ; 29 cm.
NOTE	Includes bibliographical references (p. 180–185)
SUBJECT	Retirees—United States—Statistics.
	Migration, Internal—United States—Statistics.
	Residential mobility—United States—Statistics.
LOCATION	CALL # STATUS

■ *Figure* 2.8

Library online computer screen.

In this example, the book may be used in the library but not checked out.

If your library has an open-stack policy, you can spend some time poking around the HQ1063 shelves for additional books that look promising and hopefully inspirational! In fact, if you continue to do library research in the social sciences, you will become quite familiar with the H section ("H" denotes social sciences) of the Library of Congress classification. Second letters following H denote subfields of either economics (H-HJ) or sociology (HM-HX). Books shelved under HQ, for example, deal with the family, marriage, or women. Economic theory and economic history are found under HB and HC, respectively; works on communities, class, and race are shelved under HT; and so forth. Political science is classified under J, anthropology under GN, and psychology under BF.

In addition to exploring books available in the library where you are working, you can consult catalogs of libraries other than your own by using computer networks or the Internet. For example, if your library subscribes to the online service "FirstSearch," you will be able to search a single gigantic international catalog shared by thousands of libraries ranging from the Library of Congress to Colorado College. The file to look for is called "WorldCat." The record you are shown for each item indicates exactly which libraries own it. Often smaller college libraries are part of consortiums, which allow reciprocal borrowing privileges for students at participating institutions. Groups of catalogs of individual libraries are also widely available through local networks or on the Internet. Ask your librarian to show you the best method to access them.

GOVERNMENT PUBLICATIONS AND DATA

Government reports are one source of information with which you may not have been familiar before taking courses in the social sciences. When you think about government publications, the decennial census probably comes to mind; but each year, the U.S. government publishes thousands of pages of documents covering topics ranging from the health hazards associated with smoking to the latest economic and social data. Under pressure to reduce costs, government agencies are turning to electronic publishing to replace print. Most government information may soon be available only in electronic form, primarily via the Internet, through a central standardized system of ports under www.firstgov.gov that link to all major federal government institutions to access the literally millions of reports and studies available. Print publications have been distributed in the past to a national network of official government depository libraries; these same libraries will provide the computing infrastructure needed to access electronic publications. Most large university libraries, as well as many college libraries and some larger public libraries, are government depositories. Your reference librarian will be able to identify the one nearest you and the types and amounts of documents that each repository provides.

Government documents issued in print format may or may not be entered in a library's catalog. You may instead need to rely on print or electronic versions of the *Monthly Catalog of United States Government Publications* from the Government Printing Office (GPO), which lists documents from all three branches of the federal government within a few months of their issuance date. Indexes are included each month and have been compiled annually (and often at longer intervals). From 1976 to 1995, the printed *Monthly Catalog* provided subject headings and subheadings. The 1993 cumulative index to the *Monthly Catalog* lists several entries under the heading of "Retirement." Your particular interest in retirement communities would lead you to focus on the one that reads as follows:

Retirement communities—United States—Bibliography
Retirement communities in rural America/Chen, Mingzhu (A 17 29 23), 93-27487

If you wished to pursue this bibliography on rural American retirement areas, you would look through the catalog for the entry num-

93-27487
      A 17.29:23
Chen, Mingzhu.
    Retirement communities in rural America / compiled by
Mingzhu Chen.—Beltsville, Md.: National Agricultural Library, [1993]
    viii, 36 p.; 28 cm.—(Rural Information Center publication
series,. ISSN 1056-9685; no. 23) Shipping list no.: 93-0389-P.
"April 1993."
    1. Retirement communities—United States—Bibliography.
2. Rural aged—United States—Bibliography. I. National Agricultural Library (U.S.) II. Title. III. Series. OCLC 28757078.

■ *Figure 2.9*
_____

From *Monthly Catalog*

bered 93-27487. The prefix "93-" denotes the year the item was listed
in the Monthly Catalog; the last five digits denote the sequential listing
within the year. The entry you would find appears in Figure 2.9.

    The boldface number at the top of the description (**A
17.29:23**) is the Superintendent of Documents classification number for the report. (Most depository libraries shelve documents apart
from their regular holdings; if your library has a documents collection, you should be able to find it under the section GA 1.13 of that
collection.) The first line following the classification number gives
the author of the document (e.g., Mingzhu Chen). The description
that follows does not provide you with any additional substantive
information about the bibliography, although it does tell you its
length (36 pages) and what subject headings were assigned to it. If
your library does not possess a copy of this report, your librarian
can advise you how to go about getting one.

    Beginning in 1996, the print *Monthly Catalog* has become less
useful because only keyword indexing is provided. Comprehensive
online searching, however, is possible through the GPO's federal locator service at a WWW site on the Internet. Once a publication is
identified, a link is available to locate depository libraries that receive
the publication (if it is in a print format) or to display the document
itself. The database is updated daily with preliminary records.

    The *Monthly Catalog* is only one way to search for materials
published by the federal government. Other, more specialized

guides to locating government publications are prepared by some departments of the government. For example, the U.S. Bureau of the Census—a division of the Department of Commerce—publishes a catalog of census publications, and the U.S. Bureau of Labor Statistics—a division of the Department of Labor—publishes a guide to labor statistics. *American Statistics Index* is a commercially published special index designed to help you identify the subject matter of statistical tables in government publications. *American Statistical Index,* usefully combined with indexes for both international and non–U.S. government statistics, is available on CD-ROM as part of *Statistical Masterfile.*

You need both experience and patience, as well as, often, the assistance of a librarian, to find your way through the wealth of government documents, but do not ignore them when writing research papers. They can provide valuable contextual information, as well as primary data. General Accounting Office (GAO) reports, for example, are useful at all levels of research because they are deliberately written in an approachable way, so that policymakers and their constituents can understand them.

LIBRARIES SHARING RESOURCES

For several reasons your library may not have the books, journal articles, or government publications you want. The first reason is expense. Journal subscriptions, in particular, are costly, and your library may be able to collect only the major research journals in each academic discipline. Journals that have a highly limited audience (e.g., gerontologists, demographers, or cognitive psychologists) are likely to be found only in university libraries associated with specialized graduate programs. Furthermore, even if your library currently subscribes to a journal on your list, the library may not have the issue you need. There may be gaps in the library's holdings, or state cutbacks may have severely reduced the number of journals available. Similarly, you cannot expect your library, no matter how large it is, to receive all of the books or government reports published each year.

Nonetheless, just because your library does not have what you are looking for does not mean that you should scratch a reference from your list. Because libraries are linked in a network of reciprocal borrowing, it is not necessary for each library to have everything. Many college libraries belong to local lending consortiums that allow students at one institution to use the library at another. For students, these associations allow materials to be lent out for realistic intervals; one month is the local lending period for our regional organization. If materials are not available locally, your library can probably get them from another library through the broader interlibrary loan network. With advances in computer technologies, many libraries can provide immediate full-text printouts of materials you need, or they can use online procedures to order materials from document delivery services. But as I mentioned earlier, some of these arrangements take time. You may have to travel to an unfamiliar library or wait several days to receive a book or a copy of an article through interlibrary loan. The implied message is not to give up, but to begin your library search as soon as possible.

A FINAL COMMENT: FAMILIAR TERRAIN

Regardless of the discipline, there is some degree of consensus among scholars about the major journals in their fields. There is much argument, to be sure, as to whether the research published in these journals represents the best work of these disciplines, but there is usually little doubt that scholars are at least looking at, if not reading, what is being published in these journals. Another way in which major journals may be defined is through library subscriptions; these are the journals you can expect to find in even the smallest research libraries.

Listed next are some of the major journals read by social scientists. I have included them here to give you some means of evaluating the materials you locate. An article appearing in one of these journals has been granted a certain legitimacy by its respective discipline. Several of these journals are the "official publication" of the major professional association of a discipline—for example, the American Sociological Association. Although journal articles may be too complicated for undergraduates, parts of them are approachable and are important to cite as an indication of the quality of your research. As you explore a particular topic, you will become familiar with many other journals that report research on specialized topics or subfields that cross disciplinary boundaries (e.g., *Research on Aging, Journal of Gerontology, The Gerontologist, Journal of Marriage and Family, Armed Forces and Society*).

Anthropology

American Anthropologist

American Antiquity

American Ethnologist

Anthropological Quarterly

Current Anthropology

Journal of Anthropological Research

Journal of the Royal Anthropological Institute, incorporating *Man*

Economics

American Economic Review

Journal of Economic Literature (which includes a bibliography of current articles in each issue)

Journal of Political Economy

Review of Economics and Statistics

Political Science

American Journal of Political Science

American Political Science Review

Comparative Politics

International Organization

Journal of Politics

World Politics

Political Theory

Psychology

American Psychologist

Contemporary Psychology (a journal of reviews)

Developmental Psychology

Psychological Bulletin

Psychological Review

Journal of Personality and Social Psychology

Sociology

American Sociological Review

American Journal of Sociology

Social Forces

Social Problems

Contemporary Sociology (a journal of reviews)

Valuable electronic journals are proliferating. Because many of the costs associated with producing these journals (typesetting, proofreading, printing, and binding) are eliminated, articles can appear much faster, and the number of pages is not a constraint. Also, links can be provided to display reviews of an article or to allow readers to communicate swiftly and directly with the article's author. In many cases, the electronic version of a journal closely matches a printed version. Increasingly, however, journals are available only in electronic format to take maximum advantage of the online environment. (Two examples are the *Electronic Journal of Sociology* and the *Journal of Political Ecology*.) One should be careful to evaluate the value of these newer sources; criteria such as peer review do not always occur. The previously cited organizations that advise on Internet evaluation have useful tips to quickly ascertain a journal's academic validity, such as prominent copyrights or detailed references. Internet search engines provide listings of and links to electronic journals.

RESEARCH QUESTIONS

1. Do you conduct adequate research to decide on a paper topic?

2. Do you understand the capabilities of the library, both in terms of what is available locally and how staff can help with resources such as finding specialized journals at other locations?

3. Do you follow a firm schedule for your research, ensuring that initial writing is not delayed?

4. Do you have a foolproof system for organizing information and documenting each source?

5. Do you understand the vocabulary of research, the terminology of each discipline?

6. Have you used the most appropriate and powerful search engine to find the best materials on the Internet?

7. Have you consulted social science indexes to find the best possible sources in your paper?

8. Have you been careful about your use of electronic sources, understanding the need for proper evaluation if they are not a part of an established journal or organization?

SUMMARIES AND REVIEWS OF SOCIAL SCIENCE LITERATURE

■ ■ ■

This chapter examines several kinds of writing that are based on what other social scientists have discovered. Abstracts, annotations, book reviews, and literature reviews form a hierarchy that moves from summarizing social science research to analyzing and criticizing it. Abstracts and annotations are summaries of social science research that stand on their own as finished pieces of social science writing. Book reviews range from brief summaries to larger critical analysis of a work. The analysis that book reviewing entails figures heavily into a survey of a body of research. Social scientists use these evaluative publications to efficiently access what leading research has occurred and how it has endured, so that they may build on existing knowledge in the most informed way. A review of the literature, in turn, is the foundation for a research paper in which you analyze data you collected yourself. How to organize a research paper based on original data, the next step of the process, is the topic of Chapter 4.

ABSTRACTS, ANNOTATIONS, AND OTHER SUMMARIES

Summaries of social science research appear in a number of forms. *Abstracts* found at the beginning of papers, articles, and books outline the essential elements of a work. On the basis of the abstract alone, a social science researcher often decides whether to read the abstracted article or book. *Annotations* of other people's research may appear in bibliographies, giving the reader brief information beyond that appearing in the title. Composing summaries of class materials is useful for students as well, for they can be used to prepare for an examination or class paper, long after the material was studied. Compiling these records systematically during a semester will also help process and internalize information, a concept known as writing to read.

Whether you are preparing a summary for yourself or for others, it will be useful only if it translates, as faithfully as possible, many words into few. More than any other form of social science writing, writing abstracts and other summaries requires concise language and precise usage. Most professional journals specify strict length requirements for abstracts (250 words, one or two paragraphs), and annotations are usually much shorter (five sentences or fewer). You have more latitude in preparing summaries for your own use, but you will usually find that their usefulness diminishes as their size increases. Reading one concise yet inclusive sentence will remind you of an entire chapter read months before.

Do not fall into the trap of assuming that summaries are easy-to-write, mindless exercises. To write an effective abstract or annotation, you must be able to read for the main ideas in a piece of research, recognize the relevance of these ideas for a particular audience, and organize them clearly and concisely. Although there is no rigid format for preparing summaries, you may find it useful to ask the following questions of each work.

1. *What question is posed by this work?* This central question should guide your reading of all social science literature. In a research report or journal article, this question is probably phrased in terms of some hypothesis or set of hypotheses outlining the relationship among a set of variables. For instance, "Educational attainment is affected by initial work values; it

also has socializing effects on work values and affects occupational selection" (Lindsay and Knox 1984). In a longer piece, the thesis may be stated less formally (e.g., "The debate over the role of heredity in aggressive behavior continues to rage"). Because a principal goal of your writing is economy of language, try to express the main ideas of a book or article using a vocabulary familiar to those working within a specific field. Thus, if you are investigating the effects of government regulation on the airline industry, you might want to phrase the thesis using the terminology of *organizational environments*, a concept that is well grounded in the sociological literature on organizations. Doing so not only places the research in a larger theoretical context but also makes it easier for you to compare the research with other studies that address the same general question. For undergraduates, be wary of substituting ambiguous terms for well-crafted sentences that clearly explain the meaning of the central thesis of the study.

2. *What is the method of data collection and analysis?* Readers will want to know how the major research question was investigated. Was an interview administered? Were field observations made? Were previous studies reanalyzed, or were new data collected? Was the research analyzed qualitatively (non-numerically) or quantitatively (numerically)? When and where was the research conducted? Answers to these questions place the work within broad categories of social science research and will expedite comparisons among several pieces of research.

3. *What are the findings?* Given the hypotheses to be tested, what did the researchers discover? It may be difficult to state succinctly the findings of the work you are summarizing, particularly if it is a book. Identifying the specific thesis of a book helps because the findings should address this thesis directly. Note any explicit qualifications of the results of the research, such as limitations to generalizing the results to a larger population, or the possibility that variables not measured may distort the findings.

As you begin to write the summary, do not hesitate to follow the organization of the work being summarized. For example, the chapter headings of a book or the standard format of research writing (introduction, methods, results, analysis) may provide a framework for your summary. This works well if the author's argument is organized logically and presented clearly. If not, you will want to create your own outline for organizing the summary. I suggest, however, placing the thesis in the first sentence of the summary, regardless of how the work itself is organized. Each subsequent sentence should refer in a clear way to the major idea of the work, rather than being a sequential listing of information.

Keep in mind that a summary does *not* include comments on or analysis of the material being summarized. It objectively and briefly reports the original material. You might begin your summary by identifying the author of the material, but do not introduce each sentence with something like "Smith says. . . ." It will be obvious to the reader that Smith is the author of the work being summarized. Also, quotation marks are usually not needed, as it is assumed that the summary is reporting the source directly.

Examples of Summaries

An abstract from an article appearing in a professional journal, an entry from an annotated bibliography, and a student's summary of an article for a course are shown in the following examples. Note the different style of each type of summary.

An Abstract

A Comparative Study of Working-Class Disorganization
Union Decline in Eighteen Advanced Capitalist Countries
In contrast to the diverse trends that prevailed for most of the post-war period, unionization rates in the advanced capitalist countries generally declined in the 1980s I propose a discrete-time hazard-rate

model to explain this novel pattern of labor disorganization Model estimates indicate that union decline is related to growing economic openness, unemployment, preexisting levels of unionization, the de-centralization of collective bargaining institutions, and the electoral failure of social democratic parties through the 1980s (Western 1995 179)

An Annotation

Epstein, Richard A, 1985 *Takings Private Property and the Power of Eminent Domain* Cambridge, Mass Harvard University Press

In this analysis of the eminent domain clause of the Constitution, Epstein argues that in contrast to other guarantees in the Bill of Rights, the takings clause has been interpreted quite narrowly. He contends that our system of private property and limited government is not elastic enough to accommodate the massive reforms of the New Deal, that the redistribution of wealth is not a proper role of government, and that the constitutionality of such practices as zoning, rent control, and workers' compensation is questionable (American Bar Foundation 1986 972)

A Student Summary

Thomas, Veronica   1989   "Body-Image Satisfaction Among Black Women " Journal of Social Psychology 129 107–112

This study examined body image among 102 Black women, most of whom were employed and college-educated Actual and ideal body weight, body image satisfaction, and self-esteem were examined, as were the participants' perceptions of the assessments of significant others (parents, friends, and boyfriends/spouses) Data were collected through self-administered questionnaires. Body weight was found to be inversely related to body image satisfaction, and body image satisfaction was directly related to self-esteem. The perceived assessments of close male friends and boyfriends/spouses were found to correlate most strongly with the participant's self-concept

Note that the use of the passive voice is acceptable when the same entity, the researcher or the government, would have to be monotonously repeated in the active voice.

BOOK REVIEWS

Unlike summaries, book reviews often reveal clearly what a writer thinks about a particular work—that is, they include *evaluation* In moving beyond a succinct restatement of a book's (or even an article's) main points, reviews provide a forum for the reviewer's voice and, at the same time, serve an important research function for social scientists at all levels. Professional book reviews are usually written fairly soon after a book is published, allowing scholars to keep abreast of new developments in their fields. Because they are brief (usually between 600 and 1000 words), book reviews provide a valuable guide to those conducting library research Book reviews do not simply lavish praise on some authors and hurl criticism at others; they provide a cogent summary of a work, point out both its good and bad qualities, and often place it within an established literature. Although evaluating a book within a discipline is mainly for higher level academics, students reviews should attempt to place a work within a larger academic context, citing some key related studies.

As with all types of social science writing, a book review is written for a specific audience. Knowing who will most probably read what we have written influences what we write. Some journals, such as *Contemporary Sociology* and *Contemporary Psychology,* are devoted exclusively to reviews. Written and read by specialists in various social science disciplines, the reviews in such journals assume that the readers have a good deal of background information. Journals often have book reviews after their principal articles as well. Other types—for instance, those appearing in newspapers or magazines—may make few assumptions about what potential readers know. They may, for example, have to identify a writer who is known to everyone within the profession but unknown to the general public. Because reviews for the general public can take little for granted, they may contain more summary or exposition than analysis.

Of course, just as the audience dictates what information will be included in a book review, the author's background is equally constraining. If you are not an expert in the field of family sociology, for example, you may find it difficult to write a scholarly critique of Lillian Rubin's *Worlds of Pain*. This does not mean that you could not find something informative or insightful to say about her book, just that you would probably write a review different from one by someone who teaches family sociology. You might construct an argument challenging (or supporting) the logic of Rubin's analysis, while the instructor might dwell more on the contribution of her work to the literature on family studies.

There is no formula for writing a good book review, but some guidelines can provide a foundation for writing reviews. First, do not try to cover everything in the book. True, you will want to give the reader an idea of the entire book—perhaps in a one-paragraph summary—but you can then go on to focus on its chief strengths or weaknesses, or both. For instructors, too much description rather than analysis in student reviews can indicate a lack of reflection or last-minute effort. Organize the review around the thesis of the book (and its subthesis, if relevant); avoid using the table of contents as your organizing key. *Your* thesis, that is, your interpretation of the work, provides the organizing logic of the review.

Second, support your arguments with evidence from the book. Use examples that provide the best illustrations of the points you make, trying to phrase them in your own words while retaining their contextual meaning. Reserve the use of direct quotations for those times when they are essential to making your point. If, for example, a book is especially well written (or poorly written), and you are going to comment on its style, fairness requires that you include a sample quotation or two. Sometimes only one or two direct quotes can effectively demonstrate your ideas on a book, if subsequently explicated. If you do include quotations, make them brief, and include proper citations to the book. (See the section on citation format in Chapter 7.)

Third, if you are reviewing a book in an area with which you have some familiarity, avoid using the review as an opportunity to display your own competence. Remember, readers of your review are interested in the competence of the author whose work you are reviewing, not your own. Follow closely the advice of John

Updike: "Do not imagine yourself a caretaker of any tradition, an enforcer of any party standards, a warrior in any ideological battle, a corrections officer of any kind. Review the book, not the reputation." Let the book's strengths or weaknesses speak for themselves; your review will be the stronger for it.

As a related caution, do not criticize authors because they fail to write the book you think they should have written. Identify an author's intentions and judge the merits of the book based on those intentions. Valid criticisms may be lodged against deceptive advertising, but guard against asking too much of the author. If a book purports to be an institutional analysis of educational reform, do not expect it to address the social psychological effects of curricular changes on students and teachers.

How do you go about organizing a book review? In the following, I have modified slightly a set of guidelines Barnet and Stubbs (1995) offer as a general organizing scheme for a short review, say, 500 to 1000 words:

1. An introductory paragraph identifying the work and its author, presenting the thesis of the book, and giving some indication of whether the author achieves the stated purpose of the book. This is your thesis.
2. A paragraph or two summarizing the book and relating it (where possible) to other books in this field. (This might be a slightly elaborated version of a summary of the book as described in the preceding section.) You might mention how important the work is as part of your interpretation.
3. A paragraph noting the strengths of the book (if any).
4. A paragraph noting the weaknesses of the book (if any).
5. A concluding paragraph that conveys, on balance, your assessment of the strengths and weaknesses of the book. (Does the book succeed?)

A variation on this form of social science writing is the *review essay*. Review essays are critical reviews of a book or a set of books written by experts in a particular field of study. These essays are longer than the typical review and devote more time to an assessment of the work within an established research tradition. (Often they include citations of related works.) Review essays, more than regular reviews, provide a forum for the reviewer to engage in a dialogue with the author and, consequently, lean more toward analysis than description. Reading review essays in leading newspapers is a good training ground for students who want to learn to read critically, to see how experts interpret leading books.

Examples

Reprinted next are two reviews of David Rothman's *The Discovery of the Asylum*. The first was written by a college student for a required course in writing; the second was written by a historian and appeared in a professional journal. The differences in qualifications of the reviewers and the audiences to whom they are writing should be clear as you compare these reviews.

A Student Review

ELIZABETH STONE
Writing 125

AN EXAMINATION OF ASYLUMS

The *Discovery of the Asylum* by David Rothman is a thought-provoking analysis of the origin and evolution of American institutions. Rothman describes the tumultuous events and public opinion that shaped the way deviants were treated during the eighteenth and nineteenth centuries. Using the perspective of social history, he examines the problems that developed from the decision to isolate society's misfits in asylums.

The book begins with a discussion of the treatment of deviants from the Colonial period through the Civil War. The colonists believed that deviance was the result of individual weaknesses instead of a flaw in community structure. Workhouses and almshouses were intended to discourage vagrants from invading communities and to house the poor who would "monetarily inconvenience" other residents. But in response to philosophical and practical changes—an emphasis on reason and a growing population—these practices shifted to a desire to "cure" deviants. Now, people began to search for the roots of deviance within society itself. The cure for improper behavior would be found through a system of rational codes.

It was out of this climate that the institution was born, complete with humanitarian and reformatory goals. The penitentiary, the almshouse, and the asylum were run on the principles of order, discipline, and routine. Rothman describes how ideas for the reform and rehabilitation of deviants were lost and never recovered in the blind concern for the institution's physical organization and structure. For example, in the prison system, convict labor, lack of parole, and prison crowding eventually turned the asylum into a custodial institution. "The promise of reform had built up the asylums; the functionalism of custody perpetuated them" (240).

This historical account is appealing, largely because of Rothman's style. He writes with a wry, slightly sarcastic tone, describing the ideas of the time while conveying his personal opinions. To illustrate, consider these words on corporal punishment in orphanages, a practice of which Rothman obviously did not approve: "A good dose of institutionalization could only work to the child's benefit" (209). The use of frequent quotations reinforces his historical perspective and paints a vivid picture of early American asylums. Unfortunately, Rothman fails to discuss anti-institutional movements during this time, and he offers little insight into the institutional experience from the inside. Nevertheless, Rothman's argument is well-documented. He reviews a different institution in each chapter, showing the effect of this asylum on society from its hopeful beginning to its failure.

Despite these minor shortcomings, *The Discovery of the Asylum* tells a fascinating story. These institutions were established not only to show the national government in a favorable light but also to provide a ready alternative for the accelerating disintegration of Colonial order. If we accept Rothman's argument that rehabilitation was merely a secondary consideration in the development of asylums, we must confront the question: Can the goal of curing deviance be meaningfully introduced into these institutions? Rothman's conclusions give us some hope that such a thing is possible: "We need not remain trapped in inherited answers" (295).

A Scholarly Review

Rothman, David J. 1971. *The Discovery of The Asylum: Social Order and Disorder in The New Republic*. Boston: Little, Brown.

In a book that is simultaneously a work of history and social criticism, David J. Rothman presents an interpretation of American society during the first half of the nineteenth century that is both provocative and disturbing. His thesis, which is clear and lucid, is relatively simple. By the early nineteenth century, according to Rothman, the traditional and stable society of the colonial period had begun to disintegrate. Aware of the momentous changes that were taking place, Americans were uncertain as to how they should meet the challenges of the new order and restore the social cohesion they deemed so vital to society. Obsessed with deviant and dependent behavior, they ultimately came to the conclusion that "to comprehend and control abnormal behavior promised to be the first step in establishing a new system for stabilizing the community, for binding citizens together."

The solution that Americans adopted, writes Rothman, involved the creation of the "asylum"—an institution that would reform criminals, juvenile delinquents, poor and indigent groups, mentally ill persons, and all other deviants whose abnormal behavior might or did threaten society. The result was an incredible proliferation of prisons, almshouses, houses of refuge, and mental hospitals, to cite only a few. Although most of these institutions abandoned any pretense at rehabilitation and rapidly degenerated into custodial institutions that served as "a dumping ground for social undesirables," they survived because it was easier to incarcerate undesirables than to seek new and different solutions.

While *The Discovery of the Asylum* will undoubtedly appeal to many contemporary readers who will share its author's anti-institutionalism and moral outrage, as a work of historical scholarship it leaves something to be desired. First, it indiscriminately confuses institutions that have superficial resemblances. A mental hospital—whatever its failures and shortcomings—*did* care for sick individuals, since its patient population included substantial numbers of cases of general paresis and senile psychoses (both of which were clearly of organic origin). To identify jails, almshouses, and mental hospitals as variations of one species is inaccurate, even though they had much in common. Secondly, a comparative approach casts grave doubts over the validity of Rothman's thesis. If confinement in specialized "asylums" was the response of a nation which feared change and saw institutionalization as a means of social control, how then does one explain the fact that these very same institutions (jails, almshouses, mental hospitals) appeared in England and on the continent either earlier or at the very same time as in America. Yet there is little evidence to indicate that the social order in Europe was undergoing the same or a similar process of disintegration. Thirdly, the book is simplistic; it deals with complex social processes without the subtleties and nuances that mark sophisticated scholarship. Rothman's approach to history is too rationalistic and intellectualized, for he assumes a one-to-one relationship between intent and consequence. Finally, the evidence used is either incomplete or one-sided. The book in general is not based on manuscript sources, which would have added a dimension that is presently lacking. To write about mental hospitals and yet not to examine the extensive and rich collections of Dorothea L. Dix, Thomas S. Kirkbride, Samuel B. Woodward, Pliny Earle, Edward Jarvis, and others, is unforgivable. Moreover, Rothman has conveniently summarized all of the evidence that validates his thesis, but has neglected or slighted the material that contradicts his interpretation.

I am sorry to be so critical of this book, which despite its defects has many shrewd and brilliant insights. Had Rothman not been so intent on reducing all phenomena to one simple thesis and offering a lesson to our own generation, his book could have been a major contribution to American social history. That it is not is partly a product of the confusion of ideology with scholarship.

GERALD N. GROB
Rutgers University

LITERATURE REVIEWS

Scientific research is built on previous questions others have posed and answers they have received. It points to new directions by seeking answers to previously unanswered questions, by posing questions that have yet to be asked, and by challenging answers that have been commonly accepted. In short, scientific inquiries are made in response to previous research and seek to advance our understanding of social life incrementally. For that reason, social scientists—whether professors or undergraduates—want to know what others have discovered before they begin investigations of their own.

One convenient way of finding out about previous research is to locate a literature review covering the topic that interests you. Literature reviews are critical compilations of previous research, which outline established findings, conflicting evidence, and gaps in a body of scholarship. As in abstracts and book reviews, the quality of literature reviews rests heavily on their effective summary of the work of others. Literature reviews, however, demand more of their authors than do these other forms of writing. The author must not only be familiar with a large quantity of previous research, but also be able to classify the materials and critically analyze them. To put it another way, literature reviews are exercises in writing comparisons. These exercises can be required for students in the social sciences, and the comparisons are most helpful in understanding key issues in the discipline.

Because authors of literature reviews hope to make valid comparisons among a number of related studies, they are forced to pay attention to the immense variation characterizing social science research, both between and within disciplines. One may find that two studies arrive at apparently contradictory conclusions, only to discover that the same concept (i.e., a word or phrase that represents a class of phenomena) has been measured in different ways. In one survey of published articles on poverty, for example, the authors found that the way in which "poverty" was measured determined the number of people living in substandard economic conditions (Williamson and Hyer 1975). Variation in the absolute dollar amount establishing the poverty level was one obvious source of the different results, but a number of other factors also influenced the research findings: Did the authors consider individual or family income? Were data collected in a single year or over a period of years? Were forms of public assistance included in the calculation of welfare status? This is but one example of where research investigations may share *nominal definitions* of a concept (in this example, "poverty") but rely on different *operational definitions* (ways of measuring poverty). Interpretation of terminology is a key factor in evaluating multiple studies.

Making valid comparisons in a literature review requires not only close scrutiny of how concepts are measured but also attention to many of the technical aspects of social science research. Consequently, the information you gather from each study must be more detailed than that used in preparing a review of a single book. Literature reviews begin here, with the compilation of many summaries After the results of previous research have been summarized, they must be organized and then evaluated. With the power of the Internet, both assisted by and in addition to library electronic resources, compiling comprehensive reviews is both easier and more challenging for the researcher.

Summarizing Previous Research

For each entry in the review, keep a separate outline listing each of the following.

1. *A complete bibliographic reference.* Begin each entry with a formal reference to the work being summarized. Here is an example:

```
Western, Bruce. 1995. "A Comparative Study of
Working-Class Disorganization: Union Decline in
Eighteen Advanced Capitalist Countries."
American Sociological Review 60:179-201.
```

Recording this information in standard form, or using a software program that organizes its form automatically, will save time later when you are compiling a bibliography for the review. Be careful to record all required information, such as number and volume of journals or World Wide Web URL address. Separate pages or cards will also ease the task of alphabetizing listings. (For more on bibliographic form, see Chapter 7.)

2. *The major question(s) posed in this study.* Be specific in your description of the research hypothesis of each study. If the authors explicitly state their hypothesis, record it directly, making sure to

acknowledge it as a verbatim quotation (i.e., using page number references and quotation marks). Paraphrasing and summarizing can always be done later. If your source is a book that addresses several dimensions of a widely researched concept, you may choose to focus your summary on only one or two chapters of the work. It is unlikely, for example, that you would be asked (or decide on your own) to conduct a literature review of all previous research on, say, alienation or political participation. Instead, you might wish to concentrate on the social psychological effects of alienation in the workplace.

3. *The method of investigation.* Is the study primarily qualitative or quantitative? What mode of observation was employed (e.g., questionnaires, personal interviews, field observations, archival searches)? Also, note the time frame for the study if one is given.

4. *The major variables and their operational definitions.* As mentioned previously, the way in which concepts are defined guides the findings, as well as the implications of a piece of research. Record how each variable is measured and, where possible, identify variables as *dependent, independent,* or *control. Dependent variables* are the focus of a research investigation; they denote sets of attributes that are thought to be caused by other, *independent variables.* In the hypothesis "Income varies directly with education," the dependent variable would be income, the independent variable, education. The more education a person had, the higher we would expect his or her income to be. If a dependent variable is, in fact, affected by one or more independent variables, manipulating the independent variables should result in a change in the dependent variable. If the researchers were concerned that the effect of education on income might be influenced by whether a person was African-American or European-American, they might introduce race as a *control variable.* Generally, control variables pose the question: In the presence of Z (a control variable), does the relationship between X (an independent variable) and Y (a dependent variable) change? In this example, introducing race as a control would entail comparing the relationship between education and income for European-Americans with the same relationship for African-Americans. Paying particular attention to the use of control variables is important because these

variables may qualify a general research question explored in your survey of the literature.

5. *The study population.* How is the sample of observations for this study defined? Is it composed of individuals, groups, or organizations (e.g., the family, cities, or IBM), or a collection of artifacts (e.g., newspapers, television commercials, or magazine advertisements)? Was the study conducted in this country or elsewhere? Was a method of sample selection employed in selecting a group for study? Another source of variation in research findings is the differences that arise among study populations. An obvious example is that of attitudinal surveys concerning controversial issues that are administered to different groups. Opinions regarding the legally established age limits for buying and consuming alcohol are likely to differ, depending on whether the survey is administered in a small town or a large city, at a college or a church, or to college sophomores or legislative representatives. The characteristics of the respondents or subjects are important in revealing the external validity of the research, which is the extent to which the results can be generalized to different study groups.

6. *The findings.* In describing the outcome of the research, record specific information detailing the interrelationships among the variables studied. Do not just write "Age had a significant effect on voter participation"; instead, list the magnitude and level of the effect, for example, "Age was positively correlated with voter participation ($r = 0.37$). This correlation was statistically significant at the 0.05 level." Although this type of statistical information is likely to be provided only in quantitative studies, similar care should be taken to note the particulars of qualitative findings. For example, "Regardless of their age or race, men were more likely than women to give their unsolicited opinions about the proposed change in club membership policies."

7. *The author's conclusions.* After reporting research findings, social scientists often evaluate their own analyses. They may comment on implications of their findings for future research, note the similarity between their work and previously published work, or argue that their results are similarly descriptive of other times or places. Try to record these evaluative remarks separately from your report of

the research findings because these evaluative remarks may serve as the basis for comment in your literature review. You may find that authors who present similar findings come to different conclusions, or you may decide that you object to the interpretation an author has placed on his or her data.

8. *Your comments.* Leave a place at the end of each entry to list your response to the research. While accumulating source material, you may find yourself noting similarities or differences among studies as you read them. Making a note of these observations at the time you read the study may ease the task of organizing your summaries. You may also want to use this space to jot down any reservations you have regarding the author's methods or conclusions.

Organizing the **Summaries**

Literature reviews are usually organized in one of two ways: topically or chronologically. Most often, they are structured *topically*: Previous research is divided into segments representing conceptual subsets of some larger issue. For example, a review of a concept such as alienation, which has identifiable dimensions, may logically be organized about these dimensions—for instance, powerlessness, meaninglessness, or normlessness. Similarly, reviews of a particular institution, such as the criminal courts, may be organized according to different methodologies through which they have been studied. If you are interested in judicial sentencing, for example, you may find that it makes sense to separate entries for your review into qualitative (non-numerical) and quantitative (numerical) sections. This is especially important where different methodologies have been used to ask different questions. A qualitative approach, such as making field observations in a criminal courtroom, may yield valuable insights into the dynamics between defendant and judge, but such an approach is not the best way to examine the relationship between a defendant's prior record and sentencing outcomes over a 20-year period. Investigations of the latter type are best undertaken through an archival search of court documents and lend themselves to quantitative manipulation.

The second common way of organizing literature is *chronological*. Ordering the entries in your review according to when they were published provides a historical context for your topic. If your goal is to discuss a particular concept from its emergence to its present use within a discipline, a chronological review is a useful analytical strategy. It reveals which contributions have been the most significant (in terms of repeated references by others); it points to periods of dormancy during which few researchers were working on a particular topic; and it identifies paradigmatic (major approaches) shifts in a discipline as they emerge out of well-established perspectives.

It also makes good sense to organize a review chronologically if you wish to follow the development of social science research alongside historical developments occurring *outside* its boundaries. Consider, for example, the research conducted by American sociologists on racial attitudes in this country. If you were reviewing this literature, you would not be surprised to find that questions attempting to measure race relations have varied over time. In 1940, social scientists were asking respondents whether "blacks" should be allowed to ride on the same bus with "whites"; in 1975, their surveys contained questions about busing "black" and "white" schoolchildren. How the questions were worded—substituting "black" for "Negro," for example—would also differ across the materials you encounter in your research (Schuman, Steeh, and Bobo 1985). Using a temporal framework for a review of a topic such as attitudes toward race relations can help you trace the currents of social change as they emerge and are manifested in social science research. This type of chronology often dramatically illustrates the force with which history shapes what social scientists consider worth knowing, as well as how they go about knowing it.

PREPARING A CRITICAL RESPONSE

You may have noticed from these remarks that both how summaries are prepared and how they are organized provide implicit strategies for a critical response. This means that as you get ready to write, you will probably have some sense of the major ideas that will guide your review, keeping in mind that reviews are essentially comparative exercises. In recording the same types of information for each piece of research, you will have established the basis for comparison along several lines of inquiry: purpose of the research, research methods, operationalization of major concepts, observations from different populations, discrepancies in findings, or differences in the interpretation of results. The number of comparisons you could address is probably large, but how do you go about constructing your argument?

Let's assume that you want to compare a number of studies concerned with the same hypotheses but differing in their findings. One way of proceeding is first to discuss each piece of research in turn, and then to conclude by attempting to account for the discrepancies in outcome among them. This is an effective method if the number of entries in the review is small; if you are reviewing a large body of research, your audience is likely to become mired in a catalogue of descriptions, waiting for your analysis. You can avoid this problem by selecting one or two studies that represent broadly supported findings, using these as emblematic of a group. For instance, you might write the following: "Robertson's (1972) analysis of crime in Atlanta showed that most thefts are never reported to the police." After describing this principal entry, you could follow it with something like "Smith (1983), McFarland (1966), and Jones (1985) report similar findings in their investigations of other American cities."

Try, also, to limit your descriptions of each study to the essential elements that will be used in the comparison. Provide enough information about the research to amass sufficient evidence for your analysis, but do not yield to the temptation to give long descriptive passages of each work. Each piece of research does not deserve equal (and brief) attention in your review. Length of treatment is one way to suggest whether a study is major or minor. Reserve longer summaries (and critiques) for landmark studies that inspire many others. An outline for such a literature review might be as follows:

★ I. Statement of thesis
II. Literature reviewed   *unifying*
   A. First study
   B. Second study
   C. Third study
III. Comparative analysis
   A. Similarities
   B. Differences
IV. Conclusion (in which you attempt to explain points of comparison or contrast)

An alternative strategy is to begin by describing the characteristics of research shared by several studies, and then to move to an analysis of their differences. This approach has the advantage of easily conforming to a topical structure because the generic aspects of the research—the findings, methods, and so forth—guide your analysis, rather than the discrete research investigations themselves. A corresponding outline might look like this:

★ I. Statement of thesis
II. Similarities in the research
   A. First similarity
   B. Second similarity
   C. Third similarity
III. Differences in the research
   A. First difference
   B. Second difference
   C. Third difference
IV. Conclusion (in which you reconcile similarities and differences)

Whatever type of comparative analysis you adopt, you must guide your readers through the review by beginning with a strong thesis statement. Let them know exactly how the review is organized and what your analytical strategy will be. If appropriate, specify the historical period covered in your review. Doing so at the outset may later deflect criticism that you have failed to exhaust the literature on your topic.

Here is the beginning of a literature review on the formation of the middle class in nineteenth century America:

> Increasing public concern about the effects of prevailing economic conditions on the middle class in the United States has spurred sociological interest in its historical origins and developments While current debates focus on the instability and possible decline of the middle class, the structural and cultural foundations of middle-class formation in the nineteenth century are largely obscure As yet there is no coherent middle-class history Investigations focused specifically on the historical development of the middle class are sparse, and there have been few attempts to synthesize the diverse studies of the "new" social history in terms of their relevance for understanding the middle class
>
> This review assesses social historical research relevant to the emergence and consolidation of the middle class in the nineteenth century The development of the middle class is rooted in the transformation of class and occupational structure that accompanied the growth of industrial-capitalism, rapid urbanization, immigration, and geographic mobility Key issues addressed in this review are How has the middle class been defined in sociological and historical research? What are its central features? What were the social conditions for its emergence? What are the relative importance of structural and economic conditions in shaping middle-class identity? What role did institutions play in shaping cultural values for aspirants to the middle class? (Archer and Blau 1993 18)

Extend your introductory remarks by using signposts to guide your audience through the body of your review. Use short section titles or strong transitional sentences to signify moving from one study or issue to another. Your task is to keep your reader continually aware of what the nature of the research in question is and how it relates to your central thesis (your interpretation of the research). If the review is long, provide intermediate summaries of subsections of the review. Some readers may be interested in only one or two topics covered in the review; intermediate summaries may prove helpful to their research.

As you conclude your review, make sure you go beyond a simple summary statement. Do not be afraid to give your own interpretation of this body of research. Now that you have reflected on the similarities and differences in these studies, which questions have been addressed and which have been left unanswered? What kinds of work appear more valuable in retrospect? What is the next logical step in this chain of cumulative research? What contributions might interdisciplinary work make to the research in this field? Remember that a good literature review not only reveals what social scientists have done but also serves as the foundation for future work within an established discipline.

SUMMARY QUESTIONS

1. Do you understand the utility of different sorts of summaries for social scientists?

2. Does your summary have the proper mix of analysis and description appropriate to its type? Is the summary too long to be useful?

3. Does your book review concisely examine the book's ideas without excluding key areas?

4. Have you fully considered why outcomes of similar studies are often very different?

5. Does your literature review essay effectively review a question in the discipline?

6. Is your critical response structured to give each study its appropriate emphasis?

PAPERS BASED ON
ORIGINAL RESEARCH

■ ■ ■

Research papers are the most frequently assigned type of writing in intermediate and upper-level courses in the social sciences. They require an ability to do several kinds of writing well. To write a good research paper, you must be able to summarize previous research (as you would in book reviewing), critically evaluate and compare several related studies (as you would in a literature review), and, in the end, briefly summarize a lengthy paper describing your own findings (as you would in abstracting a journal article).

All research is intended to answer a question. Consequently, research papers, regardless of their particular form, pose some problem, shape this problem into a testable hypothesis, and then report the results of the test of that hypothesis. In the social sciences, hypotheses are principally tested in two ways—through library research or through original research. The first category of research papers (often called *term papers*) relies heavily on the work of others in constructing and supporting a thesis. In this type of writing, your primary task is to organize and critically evaluate previous research on your chosen topic. The second category of papers, by contrast, describes and analyzes observations resulting from original research. Here your major focus is on the data you have collected. Research appearing in scholarly publications is used to set the context for or to supplement your own observations, but a paper of this sort chiefly presents and analyzes new data. This chapter focuses on writing papers based on original research—that is, papers of the second type; term papers involving library research are discussed in the following chapter. Most students will probably do conventional term papers first in social science classes, but because they should at least consult original research to conduct their assignment, it is vital to understand the methodology of this format.

QUANTITATIVE VERSUS QUALITATIVE RESEARCH

Social scientists make a broad distinction between two methodologies used to collect data—quantitative methodologies and qualitative methodologies. *Quantitative methodologies* are appropriate when the goal of the study is to represent some phenomenon numerically. We often associate these methods with survey research in which questionnaires—say, on smoking habits or attitudes toward democracy in Russia—are completed by respondents, or surveys are administered and the results tallied. But quantitative methods are also employed in many other types of research: studies of community crime rates, aggregate shifts in population (how many people moved, when, and where), or language and communication (how many times sexist pronouns appeared in a series of children's books), to name but a few The results of quantitative studies often assume the form of statistics (i e., summary measures describing sample outcomes). On the basis of these statistics, researchers may attempt to make inferences about the larger population from which their sample is drawn. Thanks to the Internet, sophisticated statistical information is now available to make undergraduate research more in depth, more comparable to the work of academic professionals.

Qualitative methodologies, on the other hand, are best suited to answering questions about social organization and social processes. For example, how does one "become" a marijuana user (Becker 1963), learn to identify and respond to strangers (Lofland 1985; Suttles 1968), or deal with mental illness in the context of family life (Yarrow, Schwartz, Murphy, and Deasy 1955)? Field research, in which social scientists describe and analyze the nuances of social life as they occur in some setting, is a qualitative approach frequently used by anthropologists, sociologists, and other social scientists. Qualitative researchers may, of course, report or cite quantitative studies to bolster their arguments, but they are chiefly concerned with illustrating in rich detail social interaction as it occurs in limited settings. In doing so, they develop typologies or modal categories of social action (e.g., different leadership styles) and point to the limitations of these categories as revealed in the variation among the persons they study.

Philosophical and methodological differences separate quantitative and qualitative research, and social sciences differ in their use of both types, but both kinds of research papers use basically the same format. For that reason, I discuss both types of research papers together. The major difference between qualitative and quantitative writing appears in the presentation of research findings, and it is at that point I will pause to call attention to some of their differences.

ORGANIZING THE PAPER

The most common format for organizing a paper reporting original research follows the model of hypothesis testing. This model involves the interplay between *inductive reasoning,* in which the social scientist tries to construct general principles from a set of observations, and *deductive reasoning,* in which general principles are used to explain a set of observations. Hypothesis testing is the bridge between the real world and social theory. A trained social scientist working within this framework always sees the world in terms of this question: does this example fit into a pattern or theory?

This does not mean that social scientists do not get caught up in the fascinating details of everyday life. They do; that is why they chose to study the "science" of human beings in all its richness and pathos. They may wonder why some members of their local school committee hold the opinions they do, why some women in their neighborhood enjoy being homemakers and some do not, and why some relatives are delighted with their lives in a retirement community in Florida while others are sorry they have left their old homes in Michigan. But as social scientists writing for other social scientists, they must search for a way of explaining the immense variation of social life in terms of some broader, unifying theme. School-committee voting records become data for a study of community politics, interviews with homemakers inform a study of the multiple roles available to women, and opinions about moving to Florida shed light on attitudes toward migration among the elderly. Although few social scientists may be interested in the contextual details of a specific research project, many may be eager to hear an investigator's general interpretation of these data and debate its validity, of course!

The importance of framing specific empirical observations (e.g., Mrs. Brooks plays bridge twice a week and regularly volunteers in a local hospital) in terms of some larger question (e.g., How do retired people spend their time?) carries over to how social scientists report the results of their research. Research reports appearing in scholarly journals are fairly consistent in style and tone. They tend to be formal, in that most do not use first person pronouns. ("This study explores the relationship between academic performance and career choices," rather than "I will study . . .".) This practice, however, has recently declined, and one now sometimes reads, "In this study, I explore the relationship between academic performance and career choices." Journal articles seldom contain contractions ("Women cannot . . . ," rather than "Women can't . . .") or colloquial expressions ("adolescents" rather than "teenagers").

Although not always lively, journal articles tend to be highly informative. Most, important, they usually follow a standard format. Research papers normally comprise these parts, with some latitude in their ordering:

1. Title page
2. Abstract (if appropriate)

3. Introduction/statement of problem
4. Research methodology
5. Findings/results
6. Discussion/conclusions
7. Notes (if appropriate)
8. References
9. Appendixes (if appropriate)

A research paper should always include Part 1, Parts 3 through 6, and Part 8. The other parts—abstracts, notes, and appendixes—are optional; their inclusion depends on the length of your paper, your specific needs in writing the paper, and your audience. For example, you may not need to write an abstract for a short (five- to seven-page) research paper assigned in an intermediate sociology class. But published research reports are almost all abstracted, regardless of their length.

The parts of the research paper are discussed in the order presented here, even though you probably will not write them in this order. It is unlikely, for example, that you will be able to select an appropriate title or write a good abstract before you write the body of your paper. In addition to describing each section, I illustrate each section of the original research paper with a sample student paper written by a group of four students who completed a research methods seminar with me.

THE TITLE

Good titles are difficult to construct. They tax your skills at summarizing because here, more than in any sentence you may write, every word counts. Everyone wants to begin his or her paper with a catchy title, one that will stick in a reader's head, but if you choose this route, make sure your title accurately conveys the thesis of your paper. One way to blend interest with substance is to follow a general title with a more informative subtitle. Less frequently used in journal-type writing, this pattern is frequently employed in book titles. Here are some book titles that strike me as especially memorable:

Wayward Puritans: A Study in the Sociology of Deviance

Stigma: Notes on the Management of Spoiled Identity

The Urban Villagers: Group and Class in the Life of Italian-Americans

To Dwell Among Friends: Personal Networks in Town and City

Above all, titles should be informative rather than superficial or bland. They should give enough information to convey the general, theoretical focus of the paper, as well as the specific variables that are used in the research. Try to do all this, but in the fewest words possible. Titles usually do not describe the exact setting of the research (e.g., Wellesley College, New York City, or General Motors).

1. POOR: An Analysis of Neighborhood Surveys
   IMPROVED: Attitudes Toward Racial Integration in an Urban Neighborhood
2. POOR: Staying Home
   IMPROVED: Staying Home: Suburban Homemakers Look at Themselves and Their Work
3. POOR: A Participant-Observation Study of the Fraternity Initiation Practices of Tau Kappa Epsilon at the Ohio State University
   IMPROVED: Becoming a Greek: Socialization in a Fraternal Organization
4. POOR: "There's No Business Like SNOW Business!": Boy Meets Girl at the Ski Lodge
   IMPROVED: Dating Rituals Among College Students at a Winter Resort

The original titles in the first and second examples fail to convey enough information about the research. They are so broad and unfocused that your readers will not know what to expect in your paper. The third title suffers from the opposite weakness; it is cluttered with detailed information and consequently fails to identify the general social process (in this case, socialization) of which this particular group is an example. The last title is an example of where an attempt to catch the interest of your audience backfires. In general, avoid puns; your reader may not share your sense of humor. Your title provides the first opportunity to win over your audience. Do not waste it.

Center the title in the middle of the first page of your paper. Near the bottom of the page, center your name, course number, and date. Do not number this page.

THE ABSTRACT

Because abstracts are discussed in the previous chapter, only a few words are necessary here. Your abstract, roughly 100 to 250 words, should highlight the major findings and contributions of your research. Do not include extraneous material, such as hypotheses you failed to test or sources that were of only minor relevance to your thesis. The abstract should also briefly describe the sampling procedures and methods used. Abstracts are seldom written in first person.

Throughout this chapter, I use excerpts from a student paper to illustrate the major parts of a paper based on original research. In the following abstract from that paper, note how the authors clearly and succinctly state the thesis of their paper.

What is a Liberal Arts Education?: Students' Views
and Academic Decisions

Drawing on survey data from a small, liberal arts college, this study examines the influences of educational, familial, racial, and financial background on students' curricular choices and their views of the purpose of an undergraduate education. Race, parent's educational level, and previous educational experiences all affected students' views of curriculum requirements and the purpose of an undergraduate education. However, breadth of coursework did not explain student opinions about curriculum requirements; financial aid status also failed to affect how students view their education. Because the backgrounds of students at liberal arts institutions are becoming increasingly diverse, these findings have important implications for future curriculum policies of these institutions.

THE INTRODUCTION

A good introduction sets the context for the rest of your paper by doing two things. First, it places your research within a larger disciplinary framework. It immediately signals how you intend this work to be read—that is, as following a certain theoretical, methodological, or empirical tradition (e.g., "In this study we explore reactions to drinking using an interactionist perspective"). Second, an effective introduction to a research paper offers a clear thesis statement, as well as your response to this thesis. Provide your audience with some hint as to what your conclusions will be, leaving a more complete discussion of these for the end of the paper (e.g., "We conclude that responses to public drinking are a function of social distance between the drinker and his or her audience"). All of this should be accomplished in the first few (if possible, the first one or two) paragraphs; scientific writing does not allow you time to follow a circuitous route to your thesis. It is also vital to be as clear as possible in introductions, especially for undergraduate researchers, to define your interpretation of key terms, for example. Some introductions briefly describe the research design; the subsequent research methods section will explain it fully.

Introductions are frequently organized in point–counterpoint fashion. They begin with a general statement assessing the history of research devoted to a particular topic. This generalization may focus on the type of work that has been done or on the findings from this body of work: "Students of community have long been concerned with patterns of neighborhood change . . . .”; “In the past several decades the study of deviant behavior has increasingly focused on the ‘medicalization’ of deviance . . .”; “The controversy over the viability of the nuclear family continues to rage . . .”; “Previous research indicates a great deal of consensus over the role of economic factors in migration decisions . . . .” The author then takes exception to this general assessment of the field or of a body of research, using it as a foil against which to present the thesis of the paper. The thesis may call attention to the omission of an important variable from previous research (“But few have been directly concerned with the role of X in this process”); or the thesis may challenge the assumptions of previous research (“But research to date has underestimated Weber’s depth of understanding of X”); or it may question the methods employed in previous research (“But comparative analysis based on survey results is necessarily misleading”).

This type of introduction satisfies the criteria for a good opening to a research paper; it provides immediate clues to your reader about the context and specific focus of your work. The danger in following this format is that of creating a straw man—that is, beginning with an invalid criticism of previous research to strengthen the impact of your thesis. If you write, “Introductory sociology textbooks describe the Mafia as if it were a closely knit organization controlled by a few powerful individuals. Such a picture of organized crime grossly misrepresents reality,” then you must be able to support your claim that this generalization holds for *all* introductory textbooks. Consequently, authors often qualify their initial claims to deflect potential criticisms (e.g., writing “*Many* introductory texts . . .” or “*Older* introductory texts . . .”). Your readers must agree with your assessment of a body of literature; otherwise, your introduction will create a hostile audience from the outset. Overstatement can be endemic in undergraduate writing; be careful in your use of the straw man system.

Another way of beginning a research paper is to place your specific topic within a general class of phenomena, describing how you will discuss this topic. This type of introduction is not as frequently used, largely because it does not immediately locate your research within an established body of work. It may nonetheless be an effective way of starting your paper if your focus is largely descriptive or if you are writing about a topic on which little work has been done. An ethnographic study of an urban neighborhood, for example, may offer insights concerning general patterns of social organization. The study, however, may not have been undertaken in response to omissions in previous research. (You may have been given the assignment by your research methods professor.) If something like this is the case, you need not search for a way to use the point–counterpoint construction. (Remember the pitfall of the straw man.) Instead, simply begin with a general statement that will frame the thesis of your paper, and then proceed to outline how you will support this thesis. It may be a good idea to consider this method if you are not ready to definitively confront or debate an established body of research.

Regardless of which type of opening paragraph you choose, the introduction should include a brief literature review. The review of the literature you write for a research paper is much shorter and more focused than one you would write when the sole purpose of the paper is a review of the literature on a particular topic. (See Chapter 3 for help with writing literature reviews.) When you write a literature review that stands on its own, the theme and the organization of the review flow from the broad themes you identify in the library materials you read. When you incorporate previous research into a research paper, you select the literature for its relevance to your particular thesis or set of hypotheses.

Because space limits what you can present, carefully select the literature you cite in a research paper. You will, of course, want to discuss the major studies relevant to your topic, but how do you gauge the relative significance of published research? One way is to see whether the article is often cited in the work of others. How many entries are listed below it in the *Social Sciences Citation Index* (see Chapter 2, "Using the Library and the Internet")? How many of the articles you have collected refer to it? Another way of assessing a study's significance is to look at where it was published. Did it appear in one of the leading journals in its respective discipline? (It will take you a while, of course, to get to know which journals are the leading journals.) It is important to repeat that many articles are written for a highly specialized professional audience, and the undergraduate researcher may have to look carefully for the more accessible examples. The fledgling social scientist should consult with their instructor when interpreting the relevant literature, to understand the broad parameters of the questions they raise, even if individual articles seem too formidable. Keep in mind that, aside from the scholarly significance of the research, your discussion of previous research is guided by its relevance to your specific thesis. Include only those studies that bear directly on your topic of interest.

Here is an example of an introduction, excerpted from the same undergraduate paper mentioned previously, that effectively combines a brief review of the literature with a statement of the thesis of the research.

Introduction

What constitutes a comprehensive college education? Before the curriculum reforms of the 1960s, a comprehensive education was "traditionally identified with the classical ideal of cultivation. . . . the cultivated individual has been expected to have a good appreciation and understanding of the sciences, the humanities and the arts" (Oestereicher 1991:11). However, students' demands for choice in electing courses and their desire to pursue non-Western curricula have led many universities to expand their course offerings. More recently, many college students' insistence upon receiving an education that prepares them for the workforce has transformed the goal of a college education from "an acknowledgment of academic accomplishment" to "a social credential, unrelated to competence" (Scott 1984:7). As a result of the need to offer an "academic" education and prepare students for a career, while battling increasing costs of education and competition with public universities, small liberal arts colleges must focus on "their ability to adapt to changing educational interests of students" (Breneman 1993:98).

Listening to student demands for more "practical courses" is not the only possible direction for future college curricula. Many colleges are reverting to more stringent requirements by designing a core curriculum, establishing new language requirements, and enriching Western course offerings with multicultural ones. A required, core curriculum can create a common experience for all students. Knowledge of a foreign language may help college graduates obtain jobs as well as forge an understanding between people of different cultures (Lieberman 1991). Instituting a multicultural requirement or adding a multicultural perspective to some courses teaches students about unacknowledged experiences or opinions.

This study of seniors at a small, liberal arts, women's college attempts to determine how a group of students view their educational experience and what influences both a student's opinion of the college experience and the choices she makes in her education. More specifically, we are interested in how a student's view of the purpose of a liberal arts education and how her parents' educational backgrounds determine her choice of major and general course selection. We also hope to determine how a student's race and financial pressures influence her philosophy of a liberal arts education.

Studies of students' goals for a college education show that many students are more interested in financial benefits and job training than they are in broadly expanding their knowledge (Breneman 1993; Easterlin and Crimmins 1991; Horn and Khazzoom 1993). For example, Breneman (1993: 95) found that between 1968 and 1985 the percentage of professional bachelor degrees given to students with liberal arts majors plummeted from 47% to 26%.

In addition to a desire to acquire technical training while in college, Breneman (1993) also attributed the lack of interest in liberal arts majors to an overcrowded job market, the appearance of new professional opportunities for women, and the growth of professionally-oriented academic programs in public universities.

Parental education experiences also influence student opinions about education and the scope of their academic experience. In particular, mothers' academic achievement have been found to be influential in predicting children's education achievements. Ratcliff and Jones (1990) discovered that women of a "higher ability population" at a women's college had mothers with more education than their counterparts in the "lower ability group." The educational discrepancy between first-generation college students and their parents may affect how these students interact with their parents and lead to "general cultural problems" in college (Abbott 1971; cf. London 1989). Finally, others suggest that parents who experience a growing sense of economic deprivation after 1973 encouraged their children to major in higher paying enterprises in college (Easterlin and Crimmins 1991).

The large number of college students receiving financial aid has also led researchers to question the influence of economic pressure on educational choices and degree expectations. Although one might expect financial burdens would lead students to elect majors with higher predicted earnings, St. John (1994) found that debt was not significantly related to a students choice of major. In fact, others have shown that working-class students were more likely than upper-middle class students to view a college education as an opportunity to gain general knowledge or pursue traditional liberal arts majors (Abbot 1971; Horn and Khazzoom 1993). Interestingly, students from wealthier economic backgrounds who maintained strong academic records from high school through college were more likely

to select majors with higher expected earnings;
students at private colleges, however, were
generally less likely to select majors with higher
predicted earnings (St. John 1994).

Race may also influence how college students
utilize and perceive their education. For example,
St. John (1994) reported that male Latino students
from high socioeconomic backgrounds chose profitable
majors while African-American ethnicity failed to
significantly influence a student's choice of major.
Horn and Khazzoom (1993) discovered that Asians
were more likely than Latino, Black, or white
students to aspire to an advanced degree. They also
found that Asians reported majoring in math and the
natural sciences more often than students of other
races. In addition, some studies (Ma 1989; Triandis
1989) suggest that Asian parents exert more
influence over their children's educational choices
than do parents of other ethnic backgrounds.

A few final words should be added about the importance of research hypotheses in research-paper introductions. *Hypotheses* are
propositions that represent what we expect to observe or discover in
the course of doing research. They are ideas or statements about
something that provide the focus for a study—the major concepts or
variables that will be examined—and are drawn from either personal
observation or the research of other social scientists. We usually associate hypotheses with deductive methodological approaches—that is,
with research strategies that use a general principle (stated in the form
of a hypothesis) to explain or understand a set of observations.
Hypotheses must be constructed so as to be falsifiable or potentially
proven incorrect. If our observations support our initial hypothesis,
we may claim that the hypothesis is a valid generalization; if the observations contradict our hypothesis, we must reject it in favor of
some alternative hypothesis. We must be open to the idea that our
initial ideas may have to be modified and be self-critical at every opportunity. Here again, sufficient time allows for this vital reflection.

For example, if we begin with the hypothesis that male students
are more likely than female students to make comments in classroom

settings, then we might proceed to visit a sample of classes at our university to observe the frequency of remarks by students. We might tally the number of times men speak and the number of times women speak, then compare the two frequencies. If we found that, in our sample of classes, men made 52 comments and women made 35 comments, is our initial hypothesis confirmed? Our decision regarding the hypothesis would depend on the relative numbers of men and women in each classroom. If each class were fairly evenly divided between men and women, then we have supported our general principle concerning gender differences in classroom behavior. However, if men outnumber women in many of the classrooms we observed (say, by a margin of 2.1), then our hypothesis is unsubstantiated. More comments are made by men because there are more men than women in these classes. Often in making statistical inferences, the first step in establishing a hypothesis would be to create a so-called null hypothesis whereby the independent variable is said to have no effect. The null hypothesis denies the hypothesis derived from a specific theory. To find data that supports the theory it is necessary to reject the null hypothesis. This approach guards against two types of errors: accepting that the predicted correlation exists when it does not and concluding that the predicted correlation does not exist when it does.

Hypotheses may be generally classified into three types: conditional, relational, and causal. *Conditional hypotheses* are propositions that merely assert a state of being (or condition) of someone or something (e.g., "New York City has a high crime rate"; "Voluntary associations rely on strong member commitment in order to function"; "The Democratic party in the United States has failed to articulate a coherent national platform"). Although conditional hypotheses may perform the function of motivating an argument or research strategy, they are less useful (and less often found) in social science writing than the other two types of hypotheses. In some disciplines, political science for example, might use this approach more when it attempts to predict or analyze large trends or events.

Relational hypotheses specify the relationship between two or more variables or concepts; they claim that as one variable changes, so does another, or that something is less than or more than something else. To put it another way, relational hypotheses assert the correlation between two or more things (e.g., "Both the number of functional divisions and the age of the firm are highly correlated with organizational size"; "Length of sentence varies directly with the number of previous convictions of the offender"; "Women are more likely than men to favor passage of the Equal Rights Amendment").

Causal hypotheses are a subset of relational hypotheses, in that they express a correlation between two or more variables (i.e., when X is present, Y is also present). But in addition to assuming the mutual occurrence of two factors, causal hypotheses go further to assert that one factor is responsible for the other (i.e., X causes Y). To confirm that two things are causally related, one must also be able to show that one is antecedent to the other (i.e., X preceded Y in time) and that the relationship between these two things cannot be explained away by some other factor (i.e., X and Y are not just related because of their mutual correlation with some other factor, Z). To illustrate, consider the following causal hypothesis: "Aggressive behavior among children results from watching violence on television." To substantiate this hypothesis, one would have to show that as exposure to violent television programs increases, aggressive behavior increases (correlation); that exposure to violent programs precedes the aggressive behavior (temporality); and that the correlation between exposure to violent programs and aggressive behavior is not due to some third factor, such as lack of parental supervision. If any of these conditions is questionable, then the causal relationship between television violence and aggressive behavior is called into question as well. Because of the rigorous requirements for causality, relational hypotheses are much more prevalent than causal hypotheses in social science research.

Regardless of the form of your research hypotheses, they should be stated clearly and explicitly in the introduction, as they should provide the organization for the presentation of findings and discussion that follow. The student research paper on the purposes of a liberal arts education presented six hypotheses, four of which are excerpted here. After each hypothesis, the authors provide a sentence or two elaborating the relationships they expect to find.

Hypotheses

1. Perceived quality of high school education is associated with attitudes about curriculum requirements. Students who rate highly the quality of their high school preparation in a given subject area may not see the need for a requirement in that area; students who feel they were not adequately prepared in a given area may be more likely to support a requirement in that area.

2. Breadth of college coursework will affect attitudes about curriculum requirements. Students who take a wider variety of courses will have a more positive view of requirements than those who limit their experiences to fewer subject areas. Through contact with many different disciplines, students will come to believe that a diversified course selection (as imposed by curricular requirements) is valuable.

3. Parental education will affect a student's attitude toward a liberal arts education. Parents with more education may encourage their children to acquire a general, liberal education while parents with less education will direct their children toward a more career-oriented education.

4. Financial aid status will affect a student's attitude toward a liberal arts education. Students not on financial aid may be more likely to pursue majors with higher expected earnings than students on financial aid. Students not on aid (who come from wealthier families with a higher standard of living) are more likely to be oriented toward more profitable careers.

THE RESEARCH METHODS SECTION

The methods section describes how you collected and analyzed the data for your research paper. It should be relatively detailed and provide a context for the arguments you make in the remaining sections of the paper. Whenever possible, attempt to anticipate questions that your audience might have. This section can become quite technical but it is an absolutely essential part of research. The elements discussed in the methods section include the following.

1. *The sample.* Begin by describing the units of analysis in your study. Are they individuals, collectivities (e.g., families, clubs, businesses, or communities), or artifacts (e.g., television programs, newspapers, magazines, or court cases)? Next, provide a description of your sampling procedures. How did you select your specific sample from this larger population of people, groups, or objects? If you drew a *random sample,* describe the list (e.g., a telephone or city directory, block maps, court dockets, class rosters) from which the units of analysis were selected. Finally, discuss how you selected the sample from this list (e.g., numbering each case and selecting cases using a table of random numbers; or beginning with a random start, and selecting every tenth case) If you divided your list into two or more groups before sampling (what social scientists refer to as a *stratified sample*), then state your reasons for doing so. For example, if you are interested in an attitudinal issue on which you expect men and women to hold different opinions, but your list of potential respondents contains many more men than women, you may want to use a stratified sample based on sex. In this case, using a simple random sample may not yield enough women to allow for a meaningful analysis employing sex as an independent variable.

If you do not or cannot use a random sampling technique, explain why. In general, randomness in sample selection is more important in quantitative than in qualitative studies because of the assumptions made in tests of statistical significance that allow the researcher to make inferences about some larger population using sample data. Even when randomness is not essential to the goals of your research, it is a good idea to discuss, at least briefly, the *representativeness* of your sample. For example, you might claim that you selected a particular college class for your study of teacher–student interaction because it appeared typical (in size or in proportion of male and female students) of other classes taught at this school.

State the total sample size and, if relevant, the response rate. ("Of the 100 students selected to participate in this study, 83 agreed to be interviewed.") Discuss any problems you encountered in selecting the sample and whether these lowered the level of participation in the study. Finally, briefly describe the sample in terms of characteristics significant to your investigation. If, in a study of community businesses, the age, size, and location of firms are important variables, discuss how the businesses in your sample are distributed among the categories of these variables.

2. *The measurement instrument or plan of analysis.* After describing your sample, discuss the tools you used to observe and record your data. Did you administer a questionnaire to respondents yourself, or did you mail (or e-mail) one to them? Did you conduct an interview face to face or over the phone? Was the interview structured (i.e., did you ask everyone the same questions in the same order) or unstructured (i.e., did you allow the answers given by a respondent to determine the course of the interview)? Were both open-ended and closed-ended questions included in the interview or questionnaire? How long did it take to complete a typical interview? Were there any follow-up visits for more extensive probes?

If you conducted a qualitative field study, describe what your observations consisted of. Did you keep a journal or field notes based on your observations of this group or setting? What kinds of information did you record? If you conducted a content analysis of a set of artifacts, describe what you looked for in each object in the sample and in what form these data were recorded.

Regardless of the particular methodological tool, specify how the major variable in your study is measured. For most research investigations, this will be the variable that you are trying to explain or predict—the *dependent variable*. If, for example, you designed a survey to study alienation in the workplace, you might write, "An additive index of alienation was constructed from responses to five questions, each measuring one of the dimensions of alienation defined by Seeman (1954): powerlessness, normlessness, meaninglessness, isolation, and self-estrangement. A score of five on the index represented the greatest degree of alienation; a score of zero represented the least degree of alienation." If you rely on a measurement scheme developed by someone else, be sure to acknowledge your debt—for example, "Several questions measuring powerlessness in the workplace, developed by Jones (1972), were also asked." To anticipate Chapter 8, note how the passive voice is allowed when the same entity is citing multiple studies.

The need to state clearly how the dependent variable is measured is even more imperative when you do not prescribe a fixed set of answers for it. If you use open-ended questions to measure a variable (e.g., "Why did you move to Alaska?" "What does it mean to you to feel 'at home' in a place?"), describe how you developed a coding scheme for the range of responses.

3. *The research context.* Provide any additional information necessary to ground your research in a specific context. When was your research conducted? For surveys, give the dates during which it was administered (e.g., "May through July 1987"); for observational studies, report the time of day and period of observation; for analyses of artifacts, give the time period encompassing your observations. Where was your research conducted? What role did you assume in this research (e.g., did you participate in the life of the group or did you simply observe? Were the subjects aware of your observations)? You might also forestall criticism by discussing any problems you encountered in collecting your data, such as incomplete records from which to work or an inability to observe certain behaviors. Do not feel that you have to discuss each of these elements of your research strategy in the order I have presented them. It is more important that your discussion address clearly the range of methodological issues outlined here.

The following methods section comes from the aforementioned student research paper on students' philosophies of a liberal arts education.

Research Methods

We selected our sample from a population of 487 traditionally-aged students from the class of 1995 at Wellesley College, a women's college in a suburb of Boston, Massachusetts. We interviewed only seniors because, having completed all of their course selections, they are likely to be reflecting upon their Wellesley education as they prepare to graduate.

We generated a systematic random sample of Wellesley seniors by dividing the total population by 120, selecting the first name at random, and subsequently including every fourth name. The total sample size was 122 seniors. Of this group, 94 students (77%) agreed to participate in the study. Since we did not identify any pattern among the students who did not respond or refused to participate in the study, it is unlikely that any systematic bias exists.

In particular, we thought it was important to examine the categories of two variables, race and financial aid status. The sample consisted of 55 White, 28 Asian or Southeast Asian, 2 Black, 3 Latina and 4 biracial students. Because of the small number of non-Asian minority students, we restricted racial comparisons to the first two groups. Fifty-five respondents said they received some type of financial aid, while 38 respondents said they did not. In addition, 61.7% of the respondents said that their family was the primary funding source for their Wellesley education, while 33% said that institutional financial aid was their primary funding source. With this distribution, we could complete an in-depth examination of the effect financial aid status may have on some of the dependent variables.

Our measurement instrument consisted of a seven-page interview schedule that we administered to each respondent in an interview averaging fifteen minutes. We gave respondents the option of refusing to answer any question. We asked the respondents both open- and closed-ended questions, as well as requested that they provide a list of all courses they audited or elected for credit during their

Wellesley years (including transfer, summer, abroad or other exchange credit).

We used Likert scales to measure both independent and dependent variables. The independent variables included parents' education, ranging from "less than high school" to "any graduate degree"; high school preparation in specific subject areas, ranging from "poor" to "excellent"; influence of various factors on major, minor, and elective course selection, ranging from "not at all important" to "extremely important." Our dependent variables included students' attitudes concerning a liberal arts education and attitudes concerning curriculum requirements. We measured attitudes toward a liberal arts education by asking students to rate a series of statements relating to the function of a liberal arts education. We measured attitudes toward curriculum requirements by asking a series of questions about various degree requirements at Wellesley (e.g., a writing requirement, a language requirement, a laboratory science requirement). The race of respondent was an open-ended question that we coded into several major racial categories. We concluded the interview with three closed-ended questions on financial aid status.

THE RESULTS SECTION

This section is often the largest part of a research paper. When you present your findings, you are answering the questions posed by your research hypotheses. An effective discussion section builds a strong case either in support of or in opposition to these hypotheses and sets the stage for the interpretations of the data you provide at the conclusion of your paper.

Avoid the temptation to describe your research project chronologically ("First, I did this, then, I did this"). Obviously, this is how *you* experienced it, but it is not how you should write about your research. Organize the results of your research around the hypotheses you state in your introduction. If, for example, your research hypothesis is "Career aspirations are a function of socioeconomic status, race, and sex," then discuss the results of your analysis in three sections: one in which you describe the effects of socioeconomic status on career aspirations, one in which you describe the effects of race, and one in which you describe the effects of sex.

The students writing the paper on the purpose of a liberal arts education structured their paper in this way, presenting the results of their data analysis of each of their six original hypotheses. Here is how the students presented their results about one of these hypotheses:

Results

Hypothesis 1: Perceived quality of high school education is associated with attitudes about curriculum requirements.

Depending on the particular curriculum requirement, we found different associations between perceptions of high school preparation and college degree requirements. With respect to the writing requirement, respondents who rated their high school English preparation as weak ("good" or poorer) felt that the writing requirement was very important (means of 4.25 or higher). On the other hand, respondents who rated their high school English preparation as strong ("excellent" or "very good") were somewhat less supportive of a writing requirement, as evidenced by lower mean scores (4.11 or below).

We found a different response pattern when we examined the high school language preparation in relation to attitudes about a language requirement. Those who had the weakest high school preparation were less in favor of the requirement (means of 3.75 and 3.67) than those who rated their preparation as "good" or better (means of 4.10 and above).

Finally, we observed a similar correlation of high school science preparation with the requirement of a laboratory science course. Respondents who felt their science preparation was

```
weak rated the lab requirement as unimportant (mean
of 2.50), while those who felt better prepared
rated the lab requirement as more important (means
of 3.11 and above). We note, however, that support
for this requirement is the weakest of the three
requirements discussed here, regardless of the
respondent's science preparation in high school.
```

The form in which you present your research findings depends on your methodological approach. If your study is primarily quantitative, your discussion will probably include tables or figures summarizing a large quantity of numerical information. If you use different statistical measures, such as correlations and multiple regression analysis, then discuss the results of the relationship between the variables separately for each statistical measure. If, on the other hand, your study is primarily qualitative, you will probably organize your discussion around typologies or stages in a process that emerge from your observations. Because of this difference in approach, I discuss these two types of writing separately.

Presenting Quantitative Data

Tables and figures, properly constructed, convey a large amount of information in a small space. They should enlighten, not confuse, your reader; consequently, think seriously about the best way to present them. Tables vary in format, depending on what kind of information you collect and what statistical techniques you use (e.g., frequency distributions, cross-tabulations, regressions), but the following general points are useful to keep in mind as you construct any kind of table.

1. *Provide enough information in the table so that it can be read on its own.* Number tables consecutively, and give each an appropriate title. Tables should make sense to the reader, apart from the text. The title should describe the variables that appear in the table, as well as the type of data that is being presented: "Degree of Financial Satisfaction by Gross Annual Income" (the word *by* connotes a cross-tabulation, i.e., a table containing the joint frequency distribution of

two variables); "Marital Status of Respondents in the Sample"; "Standardized and Unstandardized Regression Coefficients for Workplace Characteristics in an Equation Estimating Worker Alienation"; "Mean Levels of Education for Respondents Stratified by Sex and Hours Worked per Week." Avoid computerese in naming the variables used in the title or elsewhere in the table. It makes infinitely more sense to your audience to read "Attitudes Toward Racial Integration by Residential Neighborhood by Race" than to read "RACEINT by NEIGH by RACE."

In addition to giving clear, informative titles and variable names, explain anything that could be difficult to understand in the table. Use footnotes to explain how variables were measured or how indexes were constructed, if such matters are unclear from the title. The source of the data (e.g., survey data from a class project, census data from the U.S. Bureau of the Census) can be provided on a line at the bottom of the table. (For an illustration of source lines, refer to the hypothetical Tables 4.1–4.3 presented later in this chapter.)

2. *Standardize the format of the tables.* There is no single right way to set up tables, but try to select a format for each kind of table and stick with it throughout your paper—present all cross-tabulations using the same format, all frequency distributions using the same format, and so forth. Place each table on a separate page, and cue it into the text, using a note such as the one appearing in the following example. Then, collect the tables and append them to the end of your paper.

We were initially interested in the effect of a respondent's religious affiliation on his or her attitudes concerning a woman's legal right to an abortion. As Table 1 shows, Protestants are much more likely than either Catholics or Jews to support the legality of abortion.

3. *Discuss tables in the text; do not repeat them there.* For example, if you write, "Men constituted 55 percent of the sample, women, 45 percent," do not include a frequency distribution of sex in your paper. To do so would not tell your readers anything they didn't already know.

TABLE 4.1
Education of respondents in the sample

Education (years)	Percentage	(N)
0-11	15.5	(20)
12	34.9	(45)
13-15	25.6	(33)
16-20	24.0	(31)
Totals	100.0	(129)

SOURCE: *Garden City Community Survey, 1995.*

So what do you write about when discussing a table? The text of the discussion section should guide the reader through the tables. You might wish to point out *trends* in the table. As you move across categories of the independent variable, what happens to the dependent variable? What are the modal categories (i.e., the ones with the greatest frequencies) in the table? Or you might wish to *highlight* the more theoretically or empirically interesting findings in the table. Why are some variables in the equation statistically significant and others not? Why are almost all of the observations concentrated in the extreme diagonal corners of the table? You do not have to discuss everything that appears in a table, but you must make sure that the table, as a whole, warrants inclusion in your paper. Almost worse than repeating in the text the information in a table is including a table that you fail to mention in the text.

4. *Be selective in choosing tables to include in your paper.* Too many tables—especially those displaying findings that can be easily described in the text—will confuse and annoy your readers. A few well-chosen and properly constructed tables can provide the basis for a thoughtful and effective research paper.

CONSTRUCTING FREQUENCY DISTRIBUTIONS

A frequency distribution reports the outcome of a single variable in terms of its categories. If we wanted to construct a frequency distribution of marital status, for example, we might place everyone in the sample into one of five categories—"married," "divorced," "separated," "widowed," or "single/never married"—and then tally the number of persons in each category. The categories of variables reported in properly constructed frequency distributions are both *exhaustive* (i.e., every element in the sample is placed into some category) and *mutually exclusive* (i.e., no element is placed into more than one category). For the variable of marital status, this means that, at a given point, no one would fail to be accurately described by one of these five categories of marital status (exhaustiveness) and that no one possesses more than one of these marital statuses at one time (mutual exclusiveness). Adding the number of cases in each category results in the total sample size.

Percentage frequency distributions are created by dividing the number of scores in each category by the total sample size and then multiplying each proportion by 100. This has the result of standardizing for sample size and provides a measure more useful in analyzing the data. To return to the preceding example, knowing that 10 men and 12 women were divorced would interest a researcher only to the extent that these values represent some percentage of the total number of men and women in the sample. For that reason, a table of the distribution of a variable usually shows both the number and the percentage in each category.

One general format for displaying frequency distributions appears in Table 4.1, which shows years of education. This table shows the number of scores in each category in parentheses after the category percentages, with the total sample size (129) displayed next to the percentage total of 100 percent. An optional format would exclude the actual number in each category, as these numbers can be easily calculated by multiplying the category percentage by total sample size.

Missing data (e.g., when a respondent refuses to answer a question or when a question is left blank on a questionnaire) are not ordinarily included in the presentation of a frequency distribution. The number of responses defined as "missing" by the researcher is subtracted from the total sample size, and category percentages are then based on the remaining number of responses. An exception to this general rule is warranted when what is normally considered "missing data" is itself the subject of investigation. A substantial lack of response to a particular item on a questionnaire may indicate either that a question is difficult to understand or that it deals with an issue too sensitive to elicit a response. In these cases, you might be interested in the number of people who failed to answer the question because it might tell you something about your methodological approach.

Frequency distributions are often described in terms of two summary measures: *central tendency* and *dispersion*. Three measures of central tendency are commonly used to describe the middle of a distribution, although they differ in how that "middle" is defined. The *mode* is a frequency-based measure defined as the category with the highest number of scores. (For Table 4.1, the mode is 12 years.) The *median* is a positional measure defined as the value that divides an ordered frequency distribution into equal halves. (For Table 1, the median is 12.59 years.) The *mean* is an arithmetic measure defined as the sum of all the scores in the distribution divided by the total number of scores. (For Table 4.1, the mean is 12.95 years.)

Given that you can describe a distribution in these three ways, which statistic should you report in your paper? Your choice of an appropriate measure of central tendency is constrained by how a particular variable is measured. A median can be meaningfully interpreted only if your data can be ordered from lowest to highest. The categories of variables such as social class, political ideology, and occupational prestige can be rank ordered, but the categories of variables such as religion, ethnicity, and sex cannot. Thus, the median is an appropriate measure of central tendency for the first group of variables, but not for the second. Similarly, it does not make sense to compute a mean for a distribution unless the categories of your variable are separated by a standard unit of measurement, allowing them to be meaningfully added or subtracted from one another. Income measured in dollars or education measured in years are both examples of variables for which a mean would be a useful summary measure. Finally, a mode can be computed for any variable, as it simply represents the category with the highest number of scores.

Assuming that the data in Table 4.1 were originally measured in terms of actual number of years of education completed (before being grouped into the four categories shown here), you should probably report both the mean and the median values for the distribution. If these two statistics are close in value, the distribution is relatively symmetrical (i.e., the positional and numerical averages of the distribution coincide). If the median diverges substantially from the mean, the distribution is skewed. The mean, because it takes every score into account, will be affected by extremes in the distribution. A few high or low scores in a distribution will pull the mean up or down, respectively. The median, because it focuses only on the positional middle of the distribution, is not similarly affected by extreme scores. Because the mean (12.95) and median (12.59) in Table 4.1 are relatively close, you would not conclude that skewness was a problem in this distribution of years of education.

Measures of dispersion quantify the spread of scores about some central value in a distribution; they give us some idea as to whether the outcomes in a distribution are relatively *homogeneous* (similar in value) or relatively *heterogeneous* (different in value). The two most commonly reported measures of dispersion—*variance* and *standard deviation*—represent the scatter of scores about the mean. The variance (s^2) is computed by taking the difference of each score from the mean, squaring these differences, summing these differences over all scores, and then dividing by ($N-1$). The standard deviation (s) is simply the square root of the variance. High values for either s^2 or s mean that the scores in the distribution are widely dispersed about the mean; low values indicate a relatively tight cluster of scores about their mean. For Table 4.1, the variance is 0.66, the standard deviation 0.82. (By themselves, the numerical values of s^2 and s are difficult to interpret. When compared to other distributions used in statistical tests of hypothesis, these measures of dispersion are easier to understand.)

Measures of central tendency and measures of dispersion are either presented in the text that accompanies the table or in the table itself. If you choose to include these statistics in the table, place them at the bottom, after the frequency totals.

CONSTRUCTING CROSS-TABULATIONS

Because frequency distributions describe the outcome of a single variable, they can sometimes be introduced in the text of a research paper, eliminating the need to present the data in a table. Once you begin to examine the interrelationship of two or more variables, however, the usefulness of tables as summarizing tools greatly increases. Cross-tabulation is one of the fundamental approaches to exploring the covariation of two or more variables when each variable contains relatively few categories. The qualification "relatively few categories" is important. To illustrate, cross-tabulating a ten-category variable with another ten-category variable would yield a table of 100 cells. Not only is such a table difficult to interpret, but also, unless you have collected a tremendous amount of data, many of the cells in the table are likely to be empty. Whenever you construct a cross-tabulation that results in many empty cells, you should think seriously about regrouping your variables into fewer categories.

Suppose you are interested in the relationship between two major categories of religious preference (Protestant vs. Catholic) and two major categories of political party affiliation (Democrat vs. Republican). You might construct the cross-tabulation shown in Table 4.2, based on the results of your sample data. Table 4.2 conforms to a general format for constructing cross-tabulations: Array the independent variable across the top to establish *columns* of the table, and array the dependent variable down the side to establish *rows* of the table. Then calculate percentages *down* columns, and read *across* rows. This rule for constructing the table assumes that it makes sense to think of one variable as "dependent" and another as

TABLE 4.2
Political party affiliation by religious preference

Party affiliation	Religious preference	
	Protestant	Catholic
Democrat	58.4%	71.6%
Republican	41.6	28.4
Totals	100.0% (85)	100.0% (31)

SOURCE: *Garden City Community Survey, 1995.*

"independent." (In Table 4.2, we could justifiably argue that religious preference affects party identification, and not vice versa.) Where this is not the case, the placement of the variables is unimportant.

Does religious preference affect party identification? Reading across the row for Democrats, we find that Catholics are more likely to be Democrats than are Protestants (72% compared to 58%) and, conversely, reading across the row for Republicans, that Protestants are more likely to be Republicans than are Catholics (42% compared to 28%). Although the percentage differs between these two groups, the majority of both Catholics and Protestants are nonetheless Democrats.

These results would lead you to conclude that there is indeed an association between religious preference and party affiliation. If there were no association between these two variables, the table would have looked like Table 4.3. In Table 4.3, knowing a person's religious preference tells us nothing about his or her party affiliation. Protestants are just as likely as Catholics to be Democrats (62% of both groups); Catholics are just as likely as Protestants to be Republicans (38% of both groups). When we obtain these kinds of results, religious preference and party affiliation are said to be *statistically independent.*

A chi-square (χ^2) test for statistical independence compares the results of a table constructed from observed data (analogous to Table 4.2) to a table constructed from theoretical data that assume there is no association between the variables under consideration (analogous to Table 4.3). The details of this test would carry us beyond the purpose of illustration here. It suffices to say that if the

TABLE 4.3
Political party affiliation by religious preference

	Religious preference	
Party affiliation	Protestant	Catholic
Democrat	62.1%	62.1%
Republican	37.9	37.9
Totals	100.0% (85)	100.0% (31)

SOURCE: *Hypothetical.*

divergence between the two tables is unlikely to have resulted from chance factors (e.g., random differences in sample outcomes), then the association between the variables in the table is said to be *statistically significant.* The likelihood that a sample outcome differs from one we would expect, given no association, is represented in a probability attached to a calculated value of χ^2. In general, the larger the value of χ^2, the more likely it is that the relationship between the variables in the table is statistically significant.

To return to the illustration of religious preference and party affiliation, the calculated value of χ^2 in Table 4.2 is 16.82. The level of significance associated with this value of χ^2 is $p < 0.001$. This means that it is extremely unlikely—less than 1 in 1000—that our sample results represent random variation from a theoretical distribution assuming no association. By convention, social scientists are not willing to accept a sample outcome as statistically significant unless its probability of occurrence in a theoretical distribution of no association is less than 5 times out of 100 ($p < 0.05$). Significance levels (either 0.05, 0.01, or 0.001) are always reported alongside calculated values of χ^2 (e.g., $\chi^2 = 5.73, p < 0.05$).

Presenting Qualitative Data

The analysis of qualitative data focuses on a thorough description of the organization and varieties of some facet of social life. This does not mean that qualitative analyses ignore the frequency with which certain behaviors occur, only that they pay far more attention to the nuances of behavior that, when reported, provide a rich description of social life. How you present the findings of qualitative research depends on the goal of your research. Qualitative methods are well suited to answering many types of research questions, but they are most often used in one of three ways: (1) to identify the variation in responses to some phenomenon (e.g., the roles inmates adopt inside prisons); (2) to identify the stages in a process (e.g., how someone enters a deviant subculture); or (3) to identify the social organization of a specific group or setting (e.g., how families develop a division of labor). Regardless of the particular focus of the research, qualitative analyses strive to reveal patterns—typical ways in which things happen—in a complex set of behaviors or settings. When they succeed, these analyses often give the reader a sense of having direct experience with some aspect of social life. Such analysis may suggest that changes in the viewpoint of the reader should occur or that public policy might be reevaluated or reworked.

Identifying Response Patterns

One way to organize qualitative data is to construct a typology of responses that exhausts all of the observations you have made. This is an *inductive* approach, arriving at general patterns from the analysis of specific data. For example, Sykes and Matza (1957) were interested in how delinquents justify their deviance in terms that are not always recognized as legitimate by others. Their research resulted in a typology of five rationalizations that delinquent boys used to "neutralize" an image of themselves as deviant:

1. The denial of responsibility ("I didn't mean it").
2. The denial of injury ("I really didn't hurt anybody").
3. The denial of the victim ("They had it coming to them").
4. The condemnation of the condemners ("Everybody's picking on me").
5. The appeal to higher loyalties ("I didn't do it for myself").

This typology provides a unifying framework for describing a number of seemingly disparate responses that delinquents gave to justify their behavior. Its general utility has been seen in its extension to descriptions of rationalizations in other settings, such as the failure to vote in federal elections.

Identifying Stages in a Process

Research papers that focus on processes can often be organized chronologically. In telling your story from beginning to end, you break down what may appear to be a continuous process into critical stages or turning points in this process. You may be interested, for example, in what it means to become a member of a group, leave a community, join an interest group, or end a marriage. Although not everyone's experience will be the same, your goal is to identify the characteristics of such a process that are shared by most people you observe.

An example of this type of qualitative research is Vaughan's (1986) study of how people make transitions out of intimate relationships. From a large number of in-depth interviews with people at different points in this transition, Vaughan identified several stages in this process she refers to as "uncoupling." She argues that regardless of whether the couple were married or living together, gay or straight, one can locate pivotal points in the process of uncoupling:

1. *Secrets*—One person (the initiator) begins to feel dissatisfied with the relationship, and in response to this dissatisfaction, starts to imagine a life apart from his or her partner.
2. *The display of discontent*—The initiator defines the partner as undesirable, and in publicly conveying this information, legitimates leaving the relationship.
3. *Midtransition*—The initiator explores alternative lifestyles that might replace his or her current coupled relationship.

4. *Signals, secrecy, and collaborative cover-up*—Both partners refuse to confront directly the problems in their relationship, thereby cooperating to help each other save face.

5. *The breakdown of cover-up*—The initiator, either directly or indirectly, forces the partner to confront the troubled relationship.

6. *Trying*—The partner urges the initiator to negotiate to save the relationship; the initiator, however, may feel that he or she has already tried to remedy a bad situation.

7. *Going public*—The response of friends and family members to hearing about the troubled relationship diminishes the coupled identity and reaffirms the separate identities of the partners.

8. *The partner's transition*—The partner begins to do what the initiator has done long ago: redefine her- or himself in terms apart from the relationship.

9. *Uncoupling*—Having arrived at ways of understanding the dissolution of the relationship, both initiator and partner go on to explore their new lives and their altered relationships to others.

Although Vaughan's research focused exclusively on intimate relationships, her analysis can help us understand how people make other life-course transitions. The general stages in the process of leave-taking she identifies may appear when people leave jobs, schools, neighborhoods, churches, or families.

Identifying Social Organization

How do groups exert control over their members? How do residents define and respond to neighborhood problems? Qualitative analyses seek answers to questions such as these by describing the norms and behaviors that govern life in a particular setting. The goal of this type of research is to expose the interrelationships among actors that locate them in some system of organized activity.

In her study of communal organizations, Kanter (1972) was interested in why some utopian communities fail and others succeed. After cataloging the specific practices of a sample of utopian communities, Kanter classified these practices into six categories of "commitment mechanisms" that serve either to detach group members from a previous world or to attach them to a new community. The success of a particular utopian experiment was correlated with the group's ability to secure its membership through a number of these commitment mechanisms. Kanter's analysis yielded the following typology:

Detachment mechanisms

1. *Sacrifice*—giving up something as a requirement for membership
2. *Renunciation*—turning your back on the outside world
3. *Mortification*—stripping the identity of ties to a previous life

Attachment mechanisms

1. *Investment*—committing resources to the group, making leaving costly
2. *Communion*—emphasizing the characteristics shared by group members
3. *Transcendence*—instilling a strong ideology that stresses the importance of communal life

Like the other studies described earlier, Kanter's analysis is useful because it sheds light on a general aspect of group life—in this case, commitment. Although her data were drawn from a particular type of group, the typology of commitment mechanisms Kanter constructed from these data tell us something about how groups in general encourage a sense of belonging among their members.

Qualitative data usually consist of either field notes or direct quotations from interviews. Field notes include what you see and hear as well as your interpretation of the event. It is therefore important to dictate field notes regularly and as soon as possible after your observation or interaction. If your instructor does not give you guidelines for presenting these data, here are some suggestions you might find helpful.

1. *Indent and single space long verbatim quotations or field notes.* This format will separate your observations from your discussion of them.

2. *Provide a context for your observations.* If you are studying the interactions of members in a particular group, give some background information that will prepare your audience for your analysis. You may want to explain why and how the group started, the variation in sex, race, or class in its membership, or its relationship to other groups. If you are writing a paper in which it makes sense to include verbatim quotations, identify the respondents by social characteristics that are significant to your research. For example, if you ask people questions about how they manage neighborhood disputes, you might want to identify quotations in terms of the person's sex, age, occupation, and length of residence in the neighborhood. Make sure that you do not overidentify respondents, to the extent that their anonymity is compromised. Do not, for example, identify a quotation by a respondent's street address or specific job title (e.g., Vice President of Research and Development, Digital Corporation, Maynard, Massachusetts). Place any identifying information in parentheses at the end of the quotation:

> I really don't know when I first sensed that there was a problem with the design of the car. It might have been when the product safety supervisor started complaining about the inconsistent results of the road tests. (Male, 45, research engineer, 12 years with the company)

3. *Be selective when choosing which data to present.* Like quantitative papers that are cluttered with tables, qualitative papers that are filled with endless field notes or interviews obscure the point of your research. Choose observations for their representativeness: One

person may speak for many, or one event may illustrate many different facets of group interaction. The text can then serve as a guide to
reading your observations (as with quantitative data) by pointing
out the major themes they address.

THE DISCUSSION AND CONCLUSIONS SECTION

The final section of your paper should do two things. It should
answer the questions posed in the beginning of your paper, and it
should go beyond the particulars of your study to address the
broader significance of your research. As you sit down to write the
conclusion to your paper, ask yourself the following questions.

   1. *Were my hypotheses confirmed?* Did your sample data support
or contradict your initial research question, or—a more likely result—are your results somewhat ambiguous? Try to give a reason for
any discrepancy between your hypotheses and your results. Did your
research design—the sample you drew, the interview schedule you
used, the limits imposed by time or budgetary constraints—affect
your findings? How could these problems be avoided in the future?

   2. *What are my findings an example of?* What do these results,
based on data from some particular phenomenon, say about some
general social process? The conclusion of your paper is the appropriate place to make generalizations, when appropriate, to a larger
group or to analogous situations. For example, what does becoming
a member of a sorority say about the general process of socialization
in voluntary associations? Of what general significance are the attitudes toward abortion held by a sample of college students? What
do the interactions between customers and salesclerks in a department store reveal about the assumptions underlying economic exchange? In demonstrating your ability to think beyond your data to
make connections in analogous situations, you emphasize the
broader, theoretical importance of your research.

3. *Where do we go from here?* Having provided answers to some questions, what questions concerning your research interest remain unanswered? Research reports often conclude by briefly outlining possible directions for future research. They may suggest, for example, an alternative methodological approach to studying the same phenomenon, the inclusion of additional variables into the analysis, or the study of other settings, to see whether the results of this research can be replicated.

To return to the student research paper one last time, here is a brief section of the discussion section, in which the authors offer possible explanations for their findings concerning one hypothesis.

Discussion

Our first hypothesis—that perceptions of high school education will be correlated with attitudes about degree requirements—was confirmed, although the direction of effect varied with the type of degree requirement. In the case of writing preparation, those students who felt their English training in high school was weak were more likely to support a college writing requirement than those with better high school preparation. One explanation for this result is that students who perceive their high school education as deficient will want to improve their writing skills so that they can perform well in college. In contrast, students who felt well-prepared in high school may view a required writing course as unnecessary.

We found a different pattern for attitudes about language and laboratory science requirements. Students who believed they received weak training in a foreign language in high school were less in favor of the language requirement than those who rated their education as "good" or better. Perhaps students who have had discouraging experiences in high school language classes (or who simply feel that they "Don't have a knack for languages") may not see the benefit to college language instruction. Students who had more favorable experiences in high school, conversely, may wish to see all students share in this positive experience.

With regard to the laboratory science requirement, we found a similar direct relationship between perceived high school preparation and support for the requirement. Although the reasons for this pattern of association may be the same as we suggest above (i.e., the college laboratory requirement may be seen as the opportunity to repeat a bad high school science experience), we were most struck by the generally weak support for a lab requirement. We would hypothesize that of the three requirements we examined (writing, language, and laboratory science), students may feel that a laboratory course experience is the least applicable to their future lives. Many students may sense the importance of writing and foreign language skills beyond college, whereas laboratory science skills appear of limited value for students who do not plan to pursue scientific careers.

NOTES

If you use any notes in your research paper, number them consecutively, and append them to your paper as endnotes. Type them, double-spaced, beginning on a new page headed "Notes" (not the last page of the text of your paper). For a further discussion of the content and form of notes, see Chapter 7.

REFERENCES

Collect all references cited in your paper under the title "References," and place them at the end of the paper. Unless you are told otherwise, include only those materials you have cited in your paper. References should be alphabetized, double-spaced, and consistent in format. A guide to citation form is given in Chapter 7.

APPENDIXES

Any material that might help the reader to understand better the details of your research may be attached to your paper as appendixes. Measurement instruments (e.g., interview schedules or questionnaires) and codebooks showing how you translated your observations into categories of variables are commonly appended to research papers. Number and title each appendix. (The convention is to use Roman numerals, e.g., Appendix I, Questionnaire for Neighborhood Survey on School Integration.)

Many instructors and journals require you to place any tables or figures at the end of your paper, using a separate page for each table or figure. Number and title them, but do not paginate them.

QUESTIONS ON ORIGINAL RESEARCH PAPERS

1. How does the subject you wish to study fit into a larger pattern or field of study?

2. Have you consulted and do you understand the relevant literature when framing your investigation?

3 Does your title convey the subject of your investigation accurately and creatively?

4. Do you understand how to construct, employ, and explain the appropriate type of hypothesis?

5. Have you anticipated the questions that might be asked about your research methodology?

6. Do you fully understand the major ways that statistical findings may be measured, such as constructing cross-tabulations?

7 Do you understand the three major ways that qualitative research may be organized?

8. Does your discussion section discuss your hypothesis and place it in a broader theoretical context?

LIBRARY RESEARCH PAPERS

■ ■ ■

In contrast to papers based on original research, library research papers (sometimes called "term papers") rely on *secondary-source materials*—that is, on descriptions and analyses of social life written by others. Instead of gathering observations or administering surveys, writers of term papers conduct their fieldwork in library collections or on the Internet, although sources such as interviews with experts may be used as well. I discuss how to find your way through the library and the Internet in Chapter 2, so here I focus on how you can shape research materials you locate into an effective paper.

Writing a library research paper is not only a matter of writing; the writer is also engaged in an interactive process that alternates and combines writing and research. You will get some idea of what you want to write about—perhaps from a remark in a lecture or from something you have read in a course—and then you will search for information about it in your library. Maybe you'll take a few notes on what you find, perhaps on one of the new hand-held data collection devices. Then you will start to develop a topic and focus your library research. You return to the library for more information and take more notes, but this time you read the materials in a new, more refined way. Now you will be reading to test some ideas you have formed about a topic. When you incorporate these new materials into your paper, you may find that your thesis has changed in some important way, so you rework previous sections you had written accordingly. The point is that you do not simply go to the library, collect all the books and journals you will need, and then sit down to write. You may have to make several trips back to the library and reformulate your initial guesses about the subject several times before you are on your way to writing a coherent paper. All of this means that writing a research paper may take more time than you anticipate, so it is imperative that you get an early start. You will unknowingly be working on refining your ideas for a paper almost as soon as obtaining the first sources, so the graduate student technique of checking out sources for papers the very first week of classes is an excellent idea for everyone.

Library research papers assume a variety of forms, both in what can be said and how it is said. They may be open-ended assignments in which you explore some topic covered in a course, or they may address a particular topic specified by your instructor. If you are allowed to select your subject, you might describe some event or public issue and then attempt to analyze it using some general explanatory framework: Who supports a revision of the income tax code and why? Why did NASA decide to launch the *Challenger* space shuttle? What does the public think about the issue of "comparable worth"? What made Vaclav Havel an effective dissident but a less successful leader? Or you might write a historical analysis of a social institution: How has the Western family changed over time? What lies behind the shift from retribution to restitution in the legal system? What have been the dominant philosophies in American public education in the twentieth century? Or you might write a comparative analysis focusing on two or three subsets of some general phenomenon: Do men and women have different patterns of academic performance? How do Protestants, Catholics, and Jews compare in their attitudes toward legalized abortion? What are the major differences between Western and non-Western childrearing practices? (Of course, you will need to narrow these broad subjects into a workable topic.)

As these examples illustrate, the range of possible subjects on which you might write is immense. That is partly why research papers are such an appealing, even inspiring, type of social-science writing, but it is also what makes them potentially difficult to write well. The first step in writing a good research paper is narrowing the field of possible subjects into a single, workable topic, one that motivates you to keep investigating toward the goal of finding something worthwhile to say.

CHOOSING A TOPIC

How do you go about selecting a topic for a paper? Many stimulating questions will arise while you are taking a course or exploring a new subject, but not all of them can be developed into an effective research paper. As you develop ideas about a topic, ask yourself the following questions:

1. *Is my topic relevant to the course?* Most library research papers are assigned as a requirement for a course, and as such, they should be written with the subject matter of that course in mind. You might, for example, write about the causes of crime for both a psychology course and a sociology course, but the papers for each course would focus on vastly different library materials. As you begin to search for a topic, look at the syllabus to see what topics will be covered in the course. Spend a few hours in the library scanning the chapter headings of a textbook on the subject. If any doubts remain as to the relevance of a topic you are considering, ask your instructor or consult a discipline's web site on researching topics in social science—one can be found through the home page of the American Political Science Association, for example It is to your advantage to find out early in the term whether your interest in, say, medieval architecture is an appropriate topic, both in its subject and potential length, for your paper assignment in Sociology 313.

2. *Is my topic researchable?* You may get excited about writing a paper on some topic only to discover that there appear to be few library materials directly pertaining to your subject Some topics of current interest will not yet have made their way into the published literature of a field. Other topics may be plagued by methodological

difficulties, such as problems of access or confidentiality, limiting the amount of research published. Still other topics, such as the role of male exchange students in an exclusively female college environment, may simply not yet have been directly investigated, and, consequently, secondary sources are unavailable.

Your choice of topics need not be limited to those on which an obvious body of published work exists. It does, however, mean that you will be required to think more creatively about your particular topic in order to locate appropriate research materials in the library. You must ask yourself the question I posed about research papers in the preceding chapter—How does this example fit into a larger body of work?—because doing so may lead you to previous work that deals with analogous situations. Reading about related examples may also help you to analyze your specific example; that is, to frame it in theoretical terms that allow you to break it down into its constituent pieces, into patterns of analysis. For example, if you were writing a paper describing and analyzing the experiences of first-year college students, you might consider how entering college is similar to other transitions—starting a new job, moving to a new neighborhood, or joining a military organization. As you read research reports conducted in these other settings, you may come to see your investigation of college students as an example of socialization into new surroundings. Each social science has its own ways of categorizing, explaining, and predicting human behavior, so understanding the diverse designs of library research papers in specific disciplines can help you select a topic. Reading a newspaper article about laws to combat school violence can lead to a policy analysis paper in political science, for example. More about these forms will follow later in this chapter.

3. *Is my topic interesting?* Although you should strive to select a topic that will be interesting to your readers, you should attempt, above all, to select one that interests *you*. No matter what topic you choose, you will have to spend a considerable amount of time thinking about it, researching it, and writing about it. If you are bored with the topic, you can be sure your lack of interest will carry over

to your writing and possibly delay or diminish the quality of the final product. This doesn't mean that you should discard a subject when your initial exploration of it fails to capture your attention. It is sometimes difficult to know whether something will energize you until you have read a fair amount about it. If your initial topic interested you but is difficult to research, consider a related one that retains the inspiration of the original idea. Perhaps you are interested in the chaotic conditions in present day Russia, and in particular on rates of divorce there; however, this latter idea proves difficult to research, so you might shift to the more documented, yet still interesting, problem of failing health services.

4. *Is my topic properly defined, given the structure of the assignment?* The most difficult part of choosing a topic is finding one that can be developed into a paper appropriate in focus and length to the assignment. This entails narrowing a subject into a workable topic within the constraints of page limits imposed by course instructors or editors of scholarly publications. Suppose you were enrolled in an introductory course in sociology and were asked to write an eight- to ten-page paper about some topic listed on the syllabus. You found the section on community interesting and want to write about experiments in communal living. The subject on which you will write—"utopian communities"—is too broad in itself to serve as the topic for your paper: entire books have been written on this subject. When selecting a topic, you must narrow your focus to some aspect of "utopian communities"—for instance, why these groups were formed or how nineteenth- and twentieth-century American communes might be compared. As you begin to ask yourself what interests or what puzzles you about utopian communities, you are developing possible paper topics. Don't be discouraged if you find, as you explore your subject, that you don't fully understand everything you read about it, or that your original assumptions prove completely wrong. This can be a sign not to drop the subject, but to investigate it to creatively focus your research.

You must, of course, eventually narrow your topic to a supportable *thesis*. (But this is something you should not, or more to the point, cannot, do before you spend some time in the library researching your topic.) A thesis answers some question you pose of your topic. Let's say you begin by wondering why some communes survive while others do not. As you read about communes, you might discover that almost all nineteenth-century utopias were established in isolated, rural areas, while many twentieth-century utopias were started in the middle of large urban areas. If you find that rural communes were more likely to be self-sufficient, and that self-sufficient communes are more likely to succeed, then you have arrived at a thesis for your paper.

It is helpful to ask yourself some questions about your topic before you start your library research. You are attempting, in the language of journalism, to find an angle for your story, the point you wish to make about some specific part of a larger social issue For example, when did researchers first begin to study adolescent suicide? Why does every college senior I know want to be an investment banker? Do welfare programs affect African-American families and European-American families in the same ways? Even if you don't pursue these initial questions in your paper, they will give you some place to begin your search for relevant materials. As you look through these materials, however, don't ignore research that fails to address your specific question. You may find that you are more interested in another question that you hadn't considered at the outset.

Organizing Library Materials

Clear and logical organization is essential to writing a good library research paper. Once you have determined what form your argument will take, you are most of the way there. This is an important difference from papers based on original research. Original research reports (discussed in Chapter 4) can be organized according to the framework of hypothesis testing (i.e., statement of the problem, research methodology, and results). By contrast, library research papers can be structured in many different ways, such as compare and contrast. As you begin to consider the substance of your term paper, you should plan to spend a fair amount of time thinking about how to put it together. The organization of your paper will be guided to some extent by your subject and research traditions or approaches of each discipline. If you are writing about a specific event or issue, for example, you will have to begin by describing it in sufficient detail before you can proceed to analyze it. If you are comparing two or three instances of some phenomenon (say, three alternative educational programs), you might begin by briefly describing each, and then go on to discuss their similarities and differences. If your topic is a concept rather than a particular event, you might write about it in terms of several facets, discussing each of these in turn. A paper on the social-psychological effects of divorce, for instance, might be divided into sections that discuss the effects of divorce on the principals, their children, family members, and friends.

As you collect library materials and think about ways of organizing them, you are performing analysis, elevating your paper beyond the largely descriptive ones of your earlier academic experience. You are investigating a whole (e.g., the effects of divorce) by examining separately its several parts (e.g., the effects of divorce on couples, children, family, and friends). Of course, your analysis can succeed only if you have done a satisfactory job of constructing categories into which this information is placed. Please do not, for example, write about the library materials in the order in which you locate them, discussing the first study you comb from the library first, the second one second, and so on. (If this is your approach, you have missed the whole point of the assignment, and you could end up with an amateur research paper.) Instead, you must come up with some way of deciding that one particular study should be mentioned first, another last, and perhaps still another not at all or only in passing. As you make these kinds of decisions, you are forced to examine the interrelationships among the parts that together support your thesis and form your completed paper. Although constrained by what others have done (because you are relying on secondary-source materials), you are responsible for evaluating and organizing materials that support your argument and accounting for those that do not. Such analysis of competing materials or interpretations will be a skill useful in virtually any profession, in or out of academia.

OUTLINING

After reviewing and assembling your materials into categories, the next step is to make an initial outline. Organizing library materials in an outline allows you to determine quickly what data you have collected and what material still needs to be collected. It also helps you distinguish between major and minor issues. And, because outlining requires that you gather, in the same place, references that support the same point, it reduces the chance that your paper will be unnecessarily repetitive. After you have spent some time researching your topic in the library, sketch a broad topic outline that includes the major points you think you will cover in your paper. Let's say that in a course on organizational deviance, you have been asked to write a paper describing and analyzing a specific case of corporate misconduct. You decide to write about the charges of misleading advertising brought by the Federal Trade Commission (FTC) against Warner-Lambert company, manufacturer of Listerine. Your initial outline might look something like this:

```
  I. Background of Listerine case
 II. Suit—FTC vs. Warner-Lambert Co.
III. Sociological issues raised by case
 IV. Effects of suit on Warner-Lambert
```

BRIEF

Notice how this is a very simple plan, but it is a start to the final organization of the product. This outline suggests that you will begin with a description of the case and then move to a sociological analysis of it. In concluding, you will return to assess the impact of the case on Warner-Lambert. As you continue your library research and the focus of your paper becomes clearer, you refine and enrich your initial outline by adding subheadings under each major heading. The result is this elaborated outline:

    I. Background of Listerine case
        A. FDA drug efficacy study, 1969
        B. Focus on mouthwash producers
   II. Suit—FTC vs. Warner-Lambert Co.
        A. Notification and issuance of the complaint
        B. Administrative hearing before FTC
        C. Final order to cease and desist
        D. Appeals—U.S. Court and Supreme Court
  III. Sociological issues raised by case
        A. Administrative versus criminal law
        B. Difficulty of establishing intent
        C. Consumers as victims
        D. Organizational stigma
        E. Ambiguity of norms governing advertising
        F. Problems with the enforcement of norms
   IV. Effects of suit on Warner-Lambert
        A. Difficulty in assessing impact
        B. Economic impact on Warner-Lambert

This expanded outline highlights the major sections of the paper. From the outline alone, we would expect Section III ("Sociological issues raised by case") to be the longest and Sections I and IV ("Background of Listerine case" and "Effects of suit on Warner-Lambert") to be the shortest. (This is probably the way the paper should be constructed, with greater weight given to analysis than to description, but I'll return to that in a minute.) As you sit down to write the paper and review closely the materials you have collected, you might find it useful to do a bit of reorganization. More knowledgeable and more critical of what you are reading, you will see with increasing clarity the interrelationships among the issues you will discuss. With some revision and the addition of library references, you construct the following outline from which to write your paper:

I. Background of Listerine case
    A. FDA drug efficacy study, 1969 (<u>New York Times</u> 1969)
    B. Focus on mouthwash producers (<u>New York Times</u> 1970)
II. Suit—<u>FTC vs. Warner-Lambert Co</u>. (<u>Trade Regulation Reports</u>)
    A. Notification and issuance of the complaint
    B. Administrative hearing before FTC
    C. Final order to cease and desist
    D. Appeals—U.S. Court and Supreme Court
III. Sociological issues raised by case
    A. The nature and structure of case
        1. Administrative versus criminal law (Sutherland 1977)
        2. Difficulty of establishing intent
    B. Normative dimensions of case
        1. Ambiguity of norms governing advertising (Albion and Farris 1981; Howard and Hulbert 1973: Walsh and Schram 1980)
        2. Consumers as victims (<u>Trade Regulation Reports</u>; McGuire and Edelhertz 1980)
    C. Enforcement of the norms
        1. Problems in judicial interpretation (<u>Advertising Age</u> 1978)
        2. Overlapping jurisdiction of control agents
        3. Organizational stigma
IV. Effects of suit
    A. On Warner-Lambert (<u>Business Week</u> 1981)
    B. On the advertising community (Stotland et al. 1980)

Note that the original subheadings under Section III have been reorganized and regrouped under three new subheadings. Elaborating this section of the outline identifies several minor points of the author's analysis and reaffirms the central place of this section within the paper. Note as well that the last section of the outline has been changed to reflect the effects of the suit both on Warner-Lambert specifically and on the advertising community in general.

A few precautionary words about outlining are in order. Do not allow outlining to become a substitute for writing your paper—that is, for writing effective sentences that are organized into meaningful paragraphs, which together compose a strong research paper. You can easily spend hours constructing one outline after another (e.g., switching points B.1. and B.2., omitting point C.3), but you will not necessarily write a better paper as a result. You will know what you have to say only after you begin to write your paper (recall my remarks in Chapter 1), and you may well find that some issues you thought you would raise fit more neatly into your outline than they do into your paper. Remember that the purpose of outlining is to *guide and prepare the way for* the writing of your paper. Use an outline as a guide—not a prescription—for your writing. If, as you write, it makes sense to stray from the outline from time to time, then do so. If, on the other hand, your paper bears little resemblance to the outline, make sure that your paper still tells a logical and coherent story. (As a test, try outlining it.) With the advent of computers, with their ability to effortlessly move sentences from place to place, the need for sustained reflection about organization has become even stronger. You may be tempted to revise right out of your original and coherent structure to one that is unclear to the reader, if not yourself

BALANCE

Balance refers to the relative weight of the different parts of a paper. Compared to the number of direct quotations, how often do you summarize the work of others? Did you fill much of your paper with description and reduce the harder task of analysis? Relative to the rest of the paper, how long is the introduction? These are all questions of balance, and although there are no simple answers to these questions, they require your serious attention. The elements of a good research paper (or any paper, for that matter) are proportional to one another in such a way that the paper, as a whole, appears to be of uniform design and scale. A paper that lacks this sense of balance can cause your readers to lose sight of your general point. A three-car garage attached to a one-bedroom house is not unlike a five-page introduction to a ten-page paper. Balance can affect your writing in many ways, but here I call your attention to three aspects of balance.

1. *Balance between quotation and summary.* Because library research papers rely heavily on secondary sources, they present a strong temptation to quote library materials extensively. You can easily convince yourself that the author of a report you are reading has described the results of his or her research in the best way possible and that, consequently, you should quote the author directly. Such a conclusion is seldom justified. In incorporating the work of others into your paper, you will often find that you want to discuss or debate some points raised by an author and downplay others, or perhaps you will want to mention only briefly a point discussed extensively by an author. In these and many other instances, summary and explanation is a much more effective device than direct quotation. On the other hand, if an issue raised in a source is controversial or central to your argument, you may want to quote it directly. Be advised not to use extensive quotations as "filler" when writing last-minute papers.

You can look ahead to Chapter 7 for some advice on making decisions about when to use direct quotations. Anticipating the general message given there, you should use them sparingly. Your research paper should not read like a dialogue among published professionals in which you are a detached moderator, interjecting a transitional phrase or sentence here and there. Rather, it should read like an argument you have constructed after thoughtfully reviewing available published evidence. A few well-chosen quotations add support to your argument; too many give the impression that you haven't thought much about what you've read.

2. *Balance between description and analysis.* When instructors assign research papers, they are primarily interested in your ability to

analyze an event, an institution, or some other social phenomenon. They are less interested in your ability to describe these things. You will, of course, have to make use of description as you write your paper For example, if you were writing a paper on the aforementioned Listerine mouthwash case, you would have to describe the action brought by the FTC against Warner-Lambert: What did the FTC find misleading about the Listerine advertising campaign? What did they ask Warner-Lambert to do? How did Warner-Lambert respond? In addition, however, you need to go beyond reporting these details of the case to show that you can shape these materials into an interesting and instructive narrative. For example, what were the effects of this suit on Warner-Lambert and on the advertising industry as a whole? What does this case tell us about the nature of corporate misconduct? What does it say about the power of the federal government to control large businesses?

Although there are no strict guidelines for allocating space between description and analysis, it makes sense to follow one rule: Never spend a lot of time describing something unless you plan to analyze it, and as a corollary, spend more time describing those things that are important to your analysis. Lengthy descriptions of particular events or published research add nothing substantive to your paper; they must be supplemented by an analysis that tells your reader why these descriptive materials are important and how they relate to each other.

3. *Balance between sections of the paper.* Because they tend to be fairly long, research papers are often divided into sections through the use of subheadings. While helpful in clarifying the organization of the paper, subheadings also provide a guide to assessing balance between its various sections. They allow readers to compare the length of the descriptive and analytical sections of a paper, as well as the relationship of the introduction and conclusion to the body of the work. A 30-page paper can easily support a 3-page introduction; a 10-page paper cannot. In a long paper, you will need to give a detailed description of what is to follow, with the object of carrying the reader's interest to the end. A short paper should move more quickly to the point by means of a simply stated opening section.

The above advice is intended as general preparation for all library research papers, and the reminders listed are useful in constructing any student composition. However, there is significant variation in the structure or form of papers, and it is important for students to explore them on their own or in consultation with their instructor. For example, one form generally appropriate for social science courses is argumentation, designed to convince the reader to examine a controversial issue or perhaps debate a policy. In this format, the beginning social scientist objectively describes the controversy and then goes on to examine contending studies, giving proper space and reflection to each side. In the conclusion, one can either state which camp makes the best argument or leave that decision to the reader. Other forms are more specific to each discipline, such as social issue analysis papers in sociology or case study papers in international law. Instructors will frequently provide advice, sometimes quite emphatically, on which approach is required for the course in question, but be absolutely sure to ask if you are unsure. There are other useful forms, such as analogy or compare and contrast, which can provide increased originality and analysis to your paper. The bibliography at the end of this book lists reference works that discuss these types of papers in detail.

A STUDENT RESEARCH PAPER

Here is a research paper on the revolutionary writing of Vaclav Havel, written by a student enrolled in a political science seminar on revolutions in the modern world. This is a good paper for a number of reasons. First, it effectively blends both primary sources (Havel's own speeches, essays, and plays) and secondary sources (analyses of these speeches, essays, and plays by others), demonstrating how research papers can draw on both kinds of materials. Second, the author states a viable thesis early in the paper. By the end of the third paragraph, we know that the author will focus on how, despite his avowed denial of political interest, Havel is a spokesperson for political change, an original idea that is intriguing to explore. Third, the paper offers evidence to support this thesis in a well-organized and logical manner. Although it is somewhat unusual to see such extensive quotation from source materials in a research paper, the author provides a number of well-chosen and compelling examples—drawn from Havel's writing—to bolster her claims. (This is particularly important, given that her thesis rests on her analysis of these primary materials.) The author inserts her voice into the paper; she does not merely summarize each source cited. In evaluating this range of materials, she draws attention to some points and offers cogent summaries of others, thereby enhancing the narrative flow of the paper. Finally, she has chosen a topic that is stimulating yet reasonable in its use of available resources.

COURTNEY HAGEN
Political Science 306

Vaclav Havel: Revolutionary Writings

Vaclav Havel is an unusual revolutionary. Apart from serving as the President of the Czech Republic after the revolution of 1989, he has held no official political positions. He is not practiced in the art of guerrilla warfare; he is not known for his persuasive oratory abilities or his talent for organizing the masses. Havel claims that all he has ever wanted to do is tell the truth through his writing, that he has never had political interests, ideas, or inclinations. He first gained international recognition as a playwright, then as a champion of human rights and a dissident voice in Czechoslovakia. In 1989, he served as the moral leader of the Velvet Revolution against the Communist government in his country, despite his self-proclaimed lack of political knowledge and ideology and his status as a writer rather than a politician. [Notice how the description is exact, yet lively, with a nice transition to the thesis below.]

Yet just as Havel does not fit the profile of the typical revolutionary, he is also more than a simple playwright. His plays, letters, and essays are infused with the political beliefs he claims not to hold, full of the suggestions and ideas he argues that he never developed. The political beliefs that can be found in his writings inspired the support of the people of Czechoslovakia, captured the attention of governments in his own country and across the world, and led him down the road to revolution. [Thesis is original, intriguing in its paradoxical quality—inspiring!]

Revolutionary movements and ideas must not only point out the problems of the ancien regime, but also suggest alternative institutions and ways of living. Given this restriction, according to his own description of his writing, Havel cannot be described as a revolutionary author. He describes his theatre of the absurd style of drama as "merely a warning....[It] is not here to explain how things are. It does not have that kind of arrogance.... The absurd playwright does not have the key to anything. He does not consider himself any better informed or any more aware that his audience" (Havel 1990:54). Interestingly, he describes his role in the anti-Communist political movement in Czechoslovakia since 1968 in much the same way:

> "I've never had a clear-cut political position, much less expressed it in public. I'm a writer, and I've always understood my mission to be to speak the truth about the world I live in, to bear witness to its terrors and its miseries—in other words, to warn rather than hand out prescriptions for change. Suggesting something better and putting it into practice is a politician's job, and I've never been a politician and never wanted to be." (Havel 1990:8) [Quote illustrates thesis most elegantly, better than paraphrasing. Nice transition below.]

[handwritten margin note: Block quote then continue on w/ same ¶.]

However, close examination of his writing provides a clear picture of Havel's political beliefs and ideas and demonstrates that his analysis of his own work is not entirely accurate: throughout his plays and essays, Havel constantly provides alternatives to the political status quo.

Havel criticizes bureaucratic inefficiency in his later plays. In <u>The Memorandum</u> (Havel 1967:65), a new language is introduced to increase efficiency, but it actually proves to be cold, complicated, and alienating:

> BALLAS: Nellie! Why do you refuse to issue those damned documents?
> HELENA: Oh, for heaven's sake, love! I can't issue them until I've made sure they don't conflict with the findings in the memos, and I can't learn the findings because the blessed memos are written in Ptydepe and, as you bloody well know, I'm forbidden to make any translations whatsoever.

The play is filled with inactivity represented by the characters' repetitive language. It is set in a large office in which nothing is ever accomplished—it is never even clear what the company produces, because little production is actually achieved there. The anonymity of the setting is relevant to the message of the play, because it shows that this could be any company, any mass of inefficiency. This sort of bureaucracy, which both makes life more difficult and causes confusion in human communications, is a common target of Havel's literary arrows. [Discussion methodically yet dynamically handles different aspects of Havel's artistic commentary.]

In <u>Largo Desolato</u>, Havel examines the idea that bureaucracy and routine can be so inescapable that they can force people to do things that might violate their moral standards, or even provide a shield for immoral behavior. The police officers in the play follow orders with the complacency of automatons and cannot defend or explain their actions in any other terms. Havel (1985:31) writes:

> FIRST CHAP: Look, we've been given the job of notifying you of what we have notified you. We don't make the decisions—
> SECOND CHAP: We're small fry.

People lose sight of their own moral beliefs and lose the ability to explain their actions because the government makes it convenient to follow a routine. For fear of punishment by the government, people stop asserting their own opinions and simply follow orders. Rather than fighting against the system, they use bureaucracy as a defense for their actions, because it provides them with an easy excuse.[Appropriate balance of quote and exposition.]

In 1977, Havel gained fame as the spokesman for Charter 77, a document challenging the Czechoslovakian Communist government to follow the international human rights accords they had recently signed but continued to violate. Charter 77 enjoyed broad-based support largely because of its appeals to human rights and ethical politics. Havel claims that it was not meant to be a political document; however, it did offer an alternative lifestyle to the people and posed a real threat to the regime (Wheaton and Kavan 1992). [These scholars emphasize this key point; their inclusion makes the paper stronger.] His fight for human rights at the time drew attention to his "dissident" writing, but the theme of human dignity, equality, and respect was always an integral part of Havel's writing.

His emphasis on the importance of respect for human dignity and individuality is clear in his recommendations for the platform of an opposition party. Written at the time of the Prague Spring, when such major reforms seemed possible, "On the

Theme of an Opposition" does more than simply point out the problems with the party in power; it makes suggestions for the formation of a new kind of political party (Havel 1991a:32):

> The new party...could more quickly and radically place human individuality once more at the center of its concern, and make real individuals the measure of society and the system.... by taking an interest in concrete human lives, not distanced from their immediate and unconditional needs by ideological filters; by struggling for particular human rights, demands, and interests; by rehabilitating values that have, until recently, been considered "metaphysical," values like conscience, love of one's neighbor, compassion, trust, understanding, and so on; by redefining human dignity. [Another powerful quote, encapsulating vast issues in a succinct way.]

Human rights are so important to Havel that he believes a party based on upholding these rights would be powerful enough to pose a serious threat to the ancien regime.

According to Havel (1991b:143), the government strips people of their individualism in order to encourage mass support and involvement—the system denies individualism because individualism is a threat to the system: "Part of the essence of the post-totalitarian system is that it draws everyone into its sphere of power, not so they may realize themselves as human beings, but so they may surrender their human identity in favor of the identity of the system." [Paraphrase leads into key quote.] One of Havel's major criticisms of the Communist government is that it forces people to conform and thereby lose their unique identities. One of his earliest speeches ("On Evasive Thinking"), delivered at a writers' conference in

1965, emphasizes the importance of self-determination, even for a magazine:

> The Union of Writers ... should never hand out directives on how to write, or impose any artistic program on literature. Precisely the contrary, it must help literature and authors to be true to themselves; help magazines be what they want to be, which is the only way they will be good magazines. (Havel 1991c:19)

Charter 77 served as a way for intellectuals who disagreed with the government both to avoid entrapment by apathy and to assert their right to individualism. After the Prague Spring, the works of Havel and many other authors were banned in Czechoslovakia. The Charter provided them with a forum in which to make their opinions heard and reach out to their audiences. It allowed them to reestablish connections with the public and to do what they believed was morally correct.

Havel's writing stresses that acting according to moral beliefs is the most important action an individual can take against the government; people who do this are "living in truth" in a system that is governed by lies. He believes the government's mission is, "Not to excite people with the truth, but to reassure them with lies" (Havel 1991:66). When people accept the government as it is and believe the lies it feeds to the citizens, they may follow an easier road, but they do so at the cost of their own reason and conscience.

The lies of the system exist to blind people to its problems. Soon, the lies are so overwhelming that there develops a "blind, unconscious, irresponsible, uncontrollable and unchecked momentum that is no longer the work of the people, but which drags people along with it and therefore manipulates them" (Havel 1991b:130). People begin to believe the system and to participate in it to such an extent that they actually contribute to their own repression.

People can be harmed by the lies even if they simply refuse to fight them actively. Havel illustrates this problem in <u>Largo Desolato</u>, in which Professor Leopold Nettles is asked by representatives of the government to deny that he is the author of a controversial essay in order to win back his freedom. When they first come with the offer, he considers the idea and then sends them away. When they return, he is prepared to fight for his right to speak freely, but it is too late (Havel 1985:55):

Reproduce Inter- view

> LEOPOLD: I'm not going to sign that statement. I'd rather die than give up my own human identity—it's the only thing I've got!...
> FIRST CHAP: You don't have to sign anything! Your case has been adjourned indefinitely....
> LEOPOLD: I don't understand what it means—why don't you want my signature any more?
> FIRST CHAP: It would just be a formality. Who needs it? It's become pretty clear by now that in your case it would be superfluous—
> LEOPOLD: Are you trying to say that I'm no longer me?
> SECOND CHAP: You said it, not me.

He lost his identity because he did not engage in an active fight against the government's suggestion that he should lie about himself and his beliefs. He did not comply with them, but he did briefly consider the option, which was itself a sufficient surrender to the system of lies for him to cease to be the person he once was.

The main weapon of the government in this war against the truth is fear. It is fear that causes people to remain silent when dissident points of view that they might actually agree with are condemned by the government, fear that inspires an obedience which can become so extreme that people are led to inform on others: "In the effort to save themselves, many even report others for doing to them what they themselves have been doing to the people they report" (Havel 1991d:53).[This powerful quote illustrates the absurdity of such regimes.]

Fear and habit can force people to do things that seem far less threatening than informing on someone else, but which are nevertheless just as helpful to the system. In "The Power of the Powerless," Havel describes a greengrocer who agrees to hang a Communist slogan in his window without considering the implications of such an act. He criticizes the imaginary greengrocer's blind following of the regime, not due to the strength of the beliefs he holds, but for the sake of convenience. Although echoing the ideology of the regime in order to gain rewards and avoid punishment may seem to an individual an easy and safe sacrifice to make in order to gain peace for themselves, Havel (1991B:136) argues that they are furthering the regime's repression, whether they recognize it or not: "Individuals ... need not accept the lie. It is enough for them to have accepted their life with it and in it. For by this very fact, individuals confirm the system, fulfill the system, make the system, are the system."

People are able to live the lie because of their need to be accepted, as well as their fear of punishment by the government or their peers. The government is subtle in its manipulation. By asking people to say things that they might not have strong objections to in the first place but which still echo the ideology of the regime, it makes people believe that they have a choice in the matter, that they are not being obedient out of fear. Thanks to this manipulation, "everyone in his own way is both a victim and a supporter of the system" (Havel 1991b:144).

In "The Power of the Powerless," Havel (1991b:147) imagines what would happen if the greengrocer refused to display the government's sign: "He has enabled everyone to peer behind the curtain. He has shown everyone that it is possible to live within the truth." This, effectively, is Havel's political message: people must assert the truth by not cooperating with the unjust laws of the government. He writes that this simply follows from his moral beliefs, that it is not a political statement, but the fact that he is fighting out of an ethical responsibility and not out of political self-interest does not mean that his suggestions are not political in nature. He offers defiance as the alternative to repression under the single-party system: "The primary breeding ground for what might ... be understood as an opposition in the post-totalitarian system is living within the truth" (Havel 1991b:149). [Short quote, yet evokes much thought.]

Havel contemplated the requirements for a successful revolution and believed that one of the most important elements would be that it provides "hope of a moral reconstitution of society." His description of the necessary factors in revolution is followed by a treatise on the type of government he would like to see replace the old one. In "The Power of the Powerless," he proposes a solution to the political problems facing his country. He writes that both revolution and government restructuring should take an all-encompassing approach and should consider the needs of all levels of society. New structures put in place after the revolution must have human ties, must allow people to see, understand, and be involved with the inner workings of the system. They must also be flexible and responsive to the needs of society and develop due to demand from the people, not because they are desired by the government: "These structures should naturally arise from below as a consequence of authentic self-organization" (Havel 1991b:211). Institutions should develop quickly as new needs are discovered. Once they are no longer necessary, they should not be allowed to remain as superfluous bodies draining government resources but should be dismantled as quickly as they were created. These recommendations are not mere musings on the problems of society; they are real political solutions suggested by a keenly critical mind.

As President, Havel put his suggestions into practice nationally. He came to leadership of the country based on the people's perceptions of his strong governing abilities, his moral beliefs, and his personal popularity in Czechoslovakia, rather than as the figurehead for a new political party. In his first New Year's Day speech, he urged factories to produce only what is necessary, encouraging a streamlining of business reminiscent of his advocacy for government efficiency in "The Power of the Powerless." The speech includes other themes common to his earlier works, such as denouncing apathy, challenging everyone to take responsibility for the actions of the government by fully participating and voting, and encouraging respect for self, for other people, and for other nations.

Havel is reluctant to admit that any of his writing can be classified as political. In his interviews and essays, he claims that he has no political leanings and that his goal in writing is simply to draw his audience's attention to the truth:

> I've never taken a systematic interest in politics, political science, or economics; I've never had a clear-cut political position, much less expressed it in public. I'm a writer, and I've always understood my mission to be to speak the truth about the world I live in, to bear witness to its terrors and its miseries—in other words, to warn rather than to hand out prescriptions for change. Suggesting something better and putting it into practice is a politician's job, and I've never been a politician and never wanted to be. Even as a playwright, I've always believed that each member of the audience must sort the play out himself, because this is the only way

> his experience of it can be authentic; my job
> is not to offer him something ready-made. It
> is true that I've always been interested in
> politics, but only as an observer and a
> critic, not someone who actually does it.
> (Havel 1990:8)

As Havel's reputation for dissidence grew, people
developed political expectations of him, and the
conflict he feels about pointing out society's
problems while refusing to do anything about them
is obvious in his writings. [Good commentary on the
growth of political awareness in Havel's writings,
emphasizes evolution and progression.]

  In some of his work, he seems resentful of the
political role in which dissident writers are cast.
While he acknowledges that they volunteer their
opinions about the system and that it is therefore
not surprising that they become well-known for
their views, he feels this fame might cost
dissidents their freedom to engage in their primary
vocations. Authors can become famous politicians
without really meaning to, sometimes even without
their own interest or consent:

> The horizon of their critical attention and
> their commitment reaches beyond the narrow
> context of their immediate surroundings or
> special interests to embrace more general
> causes and, thus, their work becomes political
> in nature, although the degree to which they
> think of themselves as a directly political
> force may vary a great deal. . . . Regardless of
> their actual vocations, these people are
> talked about in the West more frequently in
> terms of their activities as committed
> citizens, or in terms of the critical,
> political aspects of their work, than in terms
> of the real work they do in their own fields.
> From personal experience, I know that there is
> an invisible line you cross—without even

wanting to or becoming aware of it—beyond
which they cease to treat you as a writer who
happens to be a concerned citizen and begin
thinking of you as a 'dissident' who almost
incidentally (in his spare time, perhaps?)
happens to write plays as well. (Havel
1991b:168)

Largo Desolato addresses this conflict in
depth. Widely believed to be autobiographical, it
portrays Professor Leopold Nettles as a dissident
writer who has just been released from prison and
is trying to avoid being sent back. While
attempting to reestablish a normal life, he is
visited by strangers and friends who remind him
that their expectations of him are high. The fans
only serve to increase Leopold's anxiety (Havel
1985:6):

> FIRST SIDNEY: There's lots of people looking
> to you—
> LEOPOLD: Thank you—
> SECOND SIDNEY: We all believe it will all turn
> out right for you in the end—
> LEOPOLD: Well, I'm not sure—
> SECOND SIDNEY: The main thing is that you
> mustn't weaken—we need you and we believe in
> you—you being the man you are—

Not only are his fans counting on him to lead them
politically, but they are also disappointed by his
limited involvement in the struggle thus far (Havel
1985:8):

> FIRST SIDNEY: You know what's best to do, after
> all you're a philosopher and I'm an ordinary
> bloke, a nobody. It goes without saying we're
> not forcing you—we haven't got the right, and
> furthermore you can't be expected to do it for
> everybody, all on your own, but, that said,
> what we think is, don't get me wrong, I'll let

you have it straight—that said, we are of the
opinion that you could be doing more than you
are in your place—

Leopold is a writer who muses on the problems
of society without necessarily suggesting concrete
changes. This is his profession, but his fans don't
believe that it's good enough anymore; without
taking action, they believe that his writing has no
purpose (Havel 1985:43):

> FIRST SIDNEY: That thing you wrote—even if we
> don't fully understand it.... and the fact that
> you're right behind it.... straight away leads
> one to hope that you will take the final step—
> LEOPOLD: What final step?
> SECOND SIDNEY: I'm not really good at
> explaining myself but let me put it like this—
> that whatever you're writing, you'll turn it
> into something that will have a practical
> effect—
> FIRST SIDNEY: To put it simply, that you'll
> come up with the pay-off to all your
> philosophizing— [The extended quotes are
> necessary to give a feeling for Havel's
> ability to demonstrate truths through art—to
> let the reader see.]

These passages raise the question of Havel's
own guilty conscience about his non-political
policies, his refusal to become more involved in
the struggle against communism than he already is,
his denial of a position of responsibility and
leadership. His situation was therefore similar to
his fictional character's. At the time that he wrote
the play, he had recently been released from
prison, and after a brief period of simply
recovering and enjoying friends and family, he
found himself under obligations and judged by the
expectations that others had of him.

Ultimately, Havel was unable to deny that he did indeed have political interests and ambitions, and that his years of observation and criticism had given him a degree of responsibility for making a change. A true revolutionary, he identified the weaknesses of the ancien regime and developed a new set of institutions with which to replace the old repressive ones that had ceased to serve the interests of the majority of citizens. In <u>Disturbing the Peace</u>, he admits that it would be difficult for a dissident writer in Czechoslovakia to avoid political involvement entirely (Havel 1990:72):

> More is expected of writers than merely writing readable books. The idea that the writer is the conscience of his nation has its own logic and its own tradition here. For years, writers have stood in for politicians; they were renewers of the national community, maintainers of the national language, awakeners of the national conscience, interpreters of the national will.

The decision to work actively to change politics rather than simply to criticize the ancien regime was a major one, but Havel acknowledges that his sense of this as the morally correct choice outweighed the disadvantages of the role (Havel 1990:xvi): *citation style*

> Occasionally ... I have this desire to cry out: 'I'm tired of playing the builder's role, I just want to do what every other writer should do, to tell the truth!' ... Or: 'Take your own risks; I'm not your savior!' But I always bite my tongue before I speak, and remind myself of what Patocka once told me: the real test of a man is not how well he plays the role he has invented for himself, but how well he plays the role that destiny assigned to him.

Havel discovered early that criticizing existing institutions carried the burden of developing recommendations for changing them as well. During his involvement with the Writers Union in the 1960s and 1970s, when he would criticize the bureaucracy of the organization, he was expected to take the responsibility for developing new statutes, since he had pointed out the problem, he didn't feel that he could deny his obligation to recommend a solution. After the collapse of the Prague Spring, he felt that he had to become more involved with the politics of Czechoslovakia; his feeling that he could no longer remain a mere observer inspired him to write his famous letter to Husak: "I got tired of always wondering how to move in this situation, and I felt the need to stir things up, to confront others for a change and force them to deal with a situation that I myself had created" (Havel 1991e:8). Not only did the letter make Havel feel that he had taken a decisive action, but it also inspired others to voice their criticisms as well.

Havel's moral strength inspired others and led them to believe in his abilities to lead them. He agreed to accept the leadership of the Civic Forum, the Velvet Revolution, and ultimately the country, because he realized that to do otherwise would be morally incorrect. He had to accept the obligations of leadership that had grown from the political nature of his writings:

> I understood the task as an extension of what I had done before—that is, a natural continuation of my former civic involvement and my activities in the revolutionary events of 1989. It simply seemed to me that, since I had been saying A for so long, I could not refuse to say B; it would have been irresponsible of me to criticize the Communist regime all my life and then, when it finally collapsed (with some help from me), refuse to

take part in the creation of something better.
(Havel 1992:xvi)

This sense of responsibility led him to what he
believed was an unlikely position—the leader of a
revolutionary movement: "I've always been put off
by revolutions. I thought of them as natural
disasters, the kind of thing that probably has to
occur once in a while in history, but it's not the
type of thing you can plan for, or get ready for,
or look forward to. And here I am, not only in a
revolution but right in the middle of it" (Havel
1990:xvii).

This position may not be where Havel expected
to find himself, but given that his writings are
filled with criticisms of the ancien regime,
political ideas, and revolutionary suggestions, it
is not surprising that this is where his political
and literary paths culminated. Havel asserts that
his writing is not political, because his purpose
is to tell the truth rather than offer solutions to
society's problems. Yet his recommendation that
people live in truth is itself a revolutionary
suggestion. It offers people the chance to avoid
the numbing effects of apathy, to assert their
individuality, and to reclaim their basic human
dignity. Despite his own arguments to the contrary,
Havel's political beliefs surface throughout his
writing, and these are the beliefs that ultimately
guided him to lead his country to revolution.

References

Brown, J.F. 1994. <u>Hopes and Shadows</u>. Durham, NC: Duke
    University Press.
Bugajski, Janusz. 1987. <u>Czechoslovakia: Charter 77's
    Decade of Discontent</u>. New York, NY: Praeger.
East, Roger. 1992. <u>Revolutions in Eastern Europe</u>.
    London: Pinter Publishers.
Garton Ash, Timothy. 1993. <u>The Magic Lantern</u>. New York,
    NY: Vintage Books.

Goldfarb, Jeffrey C. 1992. <u>After the Fall</u>. New York,
    NY: Basic Books.
Havel, Vaclav. 1991d. "Dear Dr. Husak," <u>Open Letters</u>,
    edited by Paul Wilson. New York, NY: Alfred A.
    Knopf.
——. 1990. <u>Disturbing the Peace</u>. New York, NY: Alfred
    A. Knopf.
——. 1991e. "It Always Makes Sense to Tell the Truth."
    <u>Open Letters</u>, edited by Paul Wilson. New York, NY:
    Alfred A. Knopf.
——. 1985. <u>Largo Desolato</u>. New York, NY: Grove
    Weidenfeld.
——. 1967. <u>The Memorandum</u>. New York, NY: Grove
    Weidenfeld.
——. 1991c. "On Evasive Thinking." <u>Open Letters</u>, edited
    by Paul Wilson. New York: Alfred A. Knopf.
——. 1991a. "On the Theme of an Opposition." <u>Open
    Letters</u>, edited by Paul Wilson. New York, NY:
    Alfred A. Knopf.
——. 1991b. "The Power of the Powerless," <u>Open Letters</u>,
    edited by Paul Wilson. New York, NY: Alfred A.
    Knopf.
——. 1992. <u>Summer Meditations</u>. New York, NY: Alfred A.
    Knopf.
Kriseova, Eda. 1993. Vaclav Havel: <u>The Authorized
    Biography</u>. New York, NY: St. Martin's Press.
Leff, Carol Skalnik. 1988. <u>National Conflict in
    Czechoslovakia</u>. Princeton, NJ: Princeton University
    Press.
Vadislav, Jan, ed. 1989. <u>Living in Truth</u>. London: Faber
    and Faber.
Wheaton, Bernard and Zdenek Kavan. 1992. <u>The Velvet
    Revolution</u>. Boulder, CO: Westview Press.
Whipple, Tim D., ed. 1991. <u>After the Velvet Revolution</u>.
    New York, NY: Freedom House.
Wolchik, Sharon L. <u>Czechoslovakia in Transition</u>.
    London: Pinter, 1991.

Why is this paper useful in understanding major considerations of library research papers? It achieves the proper balance of quotation to explanation and description to analysis. Although there are certainly abundant quotations, none appear without purpose and all expand on the thesis in essential, even profound, ways. The author never uses Havel's elegant words, however, without introducing their context and commenting on their meaning; the reader never has to wonder why any one selection was included. The structure of the paper also builds the case for the thesis carefully, using quotes and explanation to prove, step by step, that Havel is a major political figure despite his wishes to the contrary. Instructors would be pleased to receive and delighted to read such a paper.

LIBRARY RESEARCH PAPER QUESTIONS

1. Is your topic relevant, researchable, defined, and important to you?

2. Do you arrive at your thesis after a sustained period of investigation and reflection?

3. Do you have a series of developing outlines, each version more thoroughly organizing your evidence?

4. Are you aware of the structures or formats available for the organization of your paper or required by your instructor?

5. Do you fill your paper with quotations rather than careful summaries or paraphrases?

6. Do you introduce and then fully explain your judiciously selected quotations?

7. Are you careful to discuss your materials rather than just describe them? Do you use description merely to fill up the required pages?

ORAL PRESENTATIONS AND WRITTEN EXAMINATIONS

. . ▪

Oral presentations and written examinations, like dinner parties, require a great deal of preparation for what may seem like a brief final product. (Indeed, preparing them accounts for much of the satisfaction and benefit we derive from these activities.) Additionally, like dinner parties, talks and examinations do not normally allow for repeat performances. Once we have taken an examination or given a talk (or a party), we seldom get a chance to correct our mistakes. Consequently, oral presentations and essay examinations tend to produce inordinate amounts of anxiety. Careful preparation and practice, coupled with reasonable expectations about speaking and writing, can help alleviate the unpleasant feelings that may accompany oral presentations and examinations. They also help you to get the most out of giving a talk or taking a test, at whatever your current academic level is.

ORAL PRESENTATIONS

Faced with having to give a talk, many people can't sleep the night before, have trouble eating, drink too much coffee, and smoke cigarettes—even if they don't usually smoke. I knew a radio personality who would be physically sick before each show due to speaker's anxiety. Committing thoughts to paper may make us feel vulnerable, but at least there is some distance (in time and space) between us and the reader. When we speak, however, it is impossible to distance ourselves from our words or from our audience.

Much of the nervousness that accompanies public speaking stems from inexperience. Professors in their first semester of teaching are likely to worry much more than their seasoned colleagues about delivering class lectures. But experience explains only part of this difference. In large measure, the success of an oral presentation depends on the speaker's confidence in what he or she is doing. Your confidence will increase if you can answer "Yes" to these questions:

Is my talk interesting?

Is it focused?

Is it pitched at an appropriate level?

Is it the right length?

Do I fully understand what I'm talking about?

Have I practiced my presentation beforehand?

Facing these questions and reviewing your plans for your talk become easier the more often you prepare presentations, but they are also questions the novice speaker can—and should—confront in drafting a talk. The discussion that follows should give you some idea of how to prepare a talk, regardless of how much public speaking experience you have had.

Preparing the Talk

1. *Form.* The form of the physical material of your talk—handwritten versus typed, note cards versus typing paper, phrases versus complete sentences—depends on what works best for you. Some of my colleagues prefer to write out most of what they will say, and then practically memorize each page. Others (and I am one of these) use sketchy phrases to outline their talk, making transitions and modifications extemporaneously; this looser format also allows

more variety when the lectures are repeated in classes or to professional organizations. I also find some sort of outline helpful because it forces me to organize my talk about its main points (more on that in a minute).

Whatever approach you choose, make sure you can easily follow what you have written. Underline or highlight words and phrases, so that you won't get lost in an endless sea of words on a page. Ample margins and indentations can also help keep you on track, and you should write on only one side of the sheet or note card, as neatly as possible.

Write your talk in such a way that you are not tempted into a verbatim reading of it. Include enough information to make all of your major points, and if you can't remember an aside or a comment, write it down; don't rely on your memory. But don't be so rigid that you become flustered if you use a preposition or adjective other than the one in your notes. Allow for some discrepancy between what you have written and what you say; some of the most creative and influential things one can say are extemporaneous. Sometimes during a talk, an example will magically appear in your mind that greatly enhances your story.

2. *Audience.* Who will be attending your talk? How much will they know about your topic? What points are likely to interest them? What are their expectations for time limits or questions for your presentations? It is often difficult to arrive at straightforward answers to these questions before delivering your talk. You may not know exactly who will attend your presentation, or worse yet, you may know that the range of familiarity and interest in the topic among those in the audience will vary widely A friend of mine who recently interviewed for a faculty position at a liberal arts college was told to give a 45-minute presentation that both students and faculty members would attend. She was told that her talk should "both convey the importance of her current research to the faculty and, at the same time, be accessible and of interest to the students." Much of the anxiety she experienced before her interview concerned how she would produce a talk that would be somewhere between a paper

delivered at a professional meeting and a lecture prepared for a class of undergraduates.

My friend decided to orient her talk primarily toward the students rather than the faculty. In writing her talk, she drew on a paper she had published in a scholarly journal, but she omitted many of the technical aspects of her research (e.g., regression equations), provided additional background information and examples that did not appear in the original paper, and defined many concepts that were probably familiar to a professional audience. The decision to make some thoughtful assumptions about your audience is usually a wise one. (My friend got the job.) Your audience is there to learn something; your task is to educate, not to impress. It is often best to assume that your audience requires background information rather than leaving them possibly adrift.

A final note· Try to use examples with which your listeners can identify. When you offer an example, it should evoke a response something like "Oh, yes, that's happened to me (or to someone I know)," "I *did* feel that way," or "I remember reading about that. . . ." To illustrate, assume that you are speaking to a group of students in a college seminar about how people come to feel comfortable in new surroundings. You might introduce this idea in the following way:

```
Do you remember your first week of college? If your
experience was anything like mine, you were
probably overwhelmed by how strange everything
appeared. Your roommates, your instructors, your
dorm room, your classes—everyone and everything was
new. Being in unfamiliar territory, you had to ask
a lot of questions: Where is College Hall? Who do I
talk to about changing my course schedule? When
does the dining hall open for lunch? By the end of
the first semester, these and other questions had
become part of your taken-for-granted knowledge
about your school, and you probably had already
begun to feel that you "belonged" here by that
time. Starting college is one example of a general
```

```
process I want to talk about today: how people
become familiar with new surroundings.
```

What if you were preparing a talk on the same topic for the same audience, but instead chose the following example?

```
Do you remember your first extended vacation abroad?
If your experience was anything like mine, you were
probably overwhelmed by how strange everything
appeared. The language, the food, the customs, the
people—everything and everyone was new. Being in
unfamiliar territory, you had to ask a lot of
questions: Where is the nearest bus stop? What time
do the restaurants open for lunch? How much does a
taxi ride cost? By the end of the first couple of
weeks, these and other questions had become part of
your taken-for-granted knowledge about this
country, and you probably felt much less of a
foreigner by that time. Living abroad is one
example of a general process I want to talk about
today: how people become familiar with new
surroundings.
```

How many in your audience will share the experience described in the second example? Not many, I would guess—unless you are speaking to a group of Americans in Tokyo. The first example of starting college is much more likely to conjure up familiar images that will immediately draw your listeners into your topic. Whenever possible employ some sort of interaction, questions, or informal votes, for example, between you and the audience to give you hints of their interests and make your talk even more personal.

Selecting examples that are familiar to your audience does not exclude the possibility that your talk may elicit a response of "I hadn't thought of it in those terms before." On the contrary, ironies or counterintuitive interpretations initially unanticipated by the audience are often the major strength of a paper or presentation Relevant examples lay the foundation for these surprise endings.

3. *Content and organization.* Writing can be more subtle and complex than speaking because a reader can go back, if necessary, to reread a dense passage. To put it another way, readers exert greater control over what they read than do listeners over what they hear. Readers can regulate the tempo of the information they receive, return to passages that require a second (or third) reading, or even modify the order of what they read (Chapter 7 before Chapter 3). In contrast, listeners get only one chance to follow the argument of an oral presentation, and the statistics about people who retain much of what speakers say are decidedly grim. All of this is to say that good written essays don't necessarily make good oral presentations, and you have to take several differences into account as you begin to write your talk. Both professors and students are guilty of reading papers rather than constructing separate oral presentations, ones creatively translated from the original written work.

First, good talks usually make fewer points—and they make them with more elaborate illustrations of each point—than papers make. Many salespeople follow the maxim "keep it simple, stupid" because they know that an overly complex presentation will lose the impatient client. If you are giving a talk from a paper you have written, the best way to begin is to read it through and ask yourself. What is the point of this paper? Then, go back through a copy of the paper and highlight the passages that support or directly relate to this point. Papers are usually full of material that has little place in an oral presentation, such as complex sentences, multiple references, and methodological details. For example, in your paper you may have described four studies conducted in four different societies, all of which support the conclusion that occupations dominated by men are more highly valued than those dominated by women. In your talk, you might present one of these studies in some detail, and either omit or only briefly mention the others. Don't hesitate to purge such extraneous material; you will either have enough remaining material for the talk or you can add material (e.g., definitions of concepts with which your audience may not be familiar or extra examples to illustrate an important point) not included in your paper. Because it is easy to assume that there is only one way of saying things—the way you have already written it in your paper—writing a talk based on a paper is often more difficult than starting from scratch.

A second distinction between talks and papers centers on how you organize each one. Just as you can arrive at new ways of conveying the ideas in your paper, you can arrive at new ways of organizing them. Don't become wedded to the organization of your written paper. Your introduction may place your paper in the context of previous research through a series of citations, but this is not necessarily the best way to begin your oral presentation. For instance, the introduction to your paper might include several references to recent scholarly work on single-parent families. But when you prepare your talk, you decide instead to begin with a dramatic caricature of a parent in such a family, one that you feel illustrates the conflicting expectations and demands these parents face.

Your paper may also focus primarily on the results of your research, but you may decide it will be better to abbreviate the presentation of results and spend more time on what they mean: their interpretation and implications. The same holds true of the methods section. Your audience will usually be more interested in your data than in how the data were collected. Keep descriptions of your research methods brief, but be ready to answer methodological questions that may be prompted by your talk.

Third, organize your talk clearly and logically, and be sure to share this organization with your audience. Although it is important in your writing, it is critical in a talk that you explain where you are going and when you will get there. Your audience should know whether they are in the middle or near the end of your presentation. One way to inform your audience is to introduce your talk with a sketchy outline that gives away the punch line of your presentation. For example, "I have been spending the past several months doing research on dual-career couples. I have been particularly interested in how they manage competing work schedules alongside the constraints of raising a family. My research has led me to conclude that these couples arrive at fairly stable solutions to these difficulties, and today I want to discuss three typical patterns of managing work and family I discovered in my research. The first is. . . ." Later in your talk you can draw your audience's attention back to this organizational framework: "The second of the three patterns is . . . ," and so on. Often a written outline to be handed to the audience is invaluable, as is the newer method of computer projection of tables, pictures, and major points on a large screen.

Introductions and the rest of the presentation follow a maxim handed down to countless students of public speaking: "Tell 'em what you're going to tell 'em, tell 'em, then tell 'em what you told 'em." Such an elaboration of the major points of your thesis might be tiresomely repetitive in a piece of writing, but it is imperative when your audience can look only to you for direction. Reiterating the major points of your talk helps your audience grasp what you consider to be the heart of your presentation.

4. *Time constraints and practicing.* Just as the length of a paper—whether it is 5 pages or 25—is usually specified, so the length of a talk is usually specified. Perhaps it is to be one of three talks delivered in a 2-hour seminar, each to be followed by discussion. In this case, it would run about 20 to 25 minutes. Or perhaps it is to fill an hour. Obviously, the breadth and depth of detail of your talk depend on the time available.

Always plan a few trial runs of your oral presentation before actually giving it and carefully time yourself. Perhaps you have heard a speech that was uninspiring and most likely too long! Consider recruiting your roommate or significant other as a stand-in audience and make sure they have a watch. In general, you speak more rapidly when you deliver your talk than when you practice it. (One response to being nervous is to accelerate your rate of speaking.) If your talk is typewritten, double-spaced, allow about two minutes per page in presenting it. Notes consisting of phrases will vary in delivery time, depending on how cryptic they are and on whether you allow for questions during your presentation. Most speakers allow some time (roughly 10 minutes) for questions either during or after their talk and can be invaluable in connecting to your audience. Leaving time for two-way communication gives listeners a feeling of respect for their time and opinions.

5. *Style.* Be conversational. Research papers, even when they contain highly technical material, are intelligible because readers can read through them at their own pace, slowing down to chew and digest the difficult thoughts. Oral presentations, however, have to be caught on the wing, so you should avoid complicated language, concepts, and results that need a lot of explanation. Try to use language that can be easily grasped the first time around. Don't hesitate to use first-person pronouns. In searching for models of effective presentations, think about what you liked or disliked about talks or class lectures you have heard. Consider the idea of "teaching by delight" and occasionally incorporate humor and vibrant examples, anything to stimulate your group. There is always a balance between indulging the audience and recounting complicated ideas; it is your job to find that key point.

If statistical materials are an integral part of your talk, bring along copies of tables or graphs that can be distributed to your audience, or prepare transparencies of these that can be used on an overhead projector. Keep such illustrations to a minimum, however; you want your audience to be listening to you, not reading your materials. An alternative to distributing materials during your talk is to offer them at the end. (You might say something like, "I have copies of these materials if anyone would like to see them at the conclusion of my talk.") If a simple visual image of something is all that is needed, draw it on the board or use computer projection technology. This helps punctuate your talk as well as clarify any misunderstanding that might arise out of a verbal description.

Giving the Talk

1. *Fluency.* Nervousness is part of speaking, but you can reduce its negative influence over time. You will be—most of us are—nervous, and a little nervousness may help you give a good

presentation. (Professors who deliver the same lecture for the tenth time often perform poorly because they are not nervous enough.) If you are too nervous, though, you may speak too quickly or distract your audience with an annoying gesture, such as tapping your foot, swaying from side to side, or shuffling your papers. Taking a few deep breaths before you begin helps. So does making a conscious effort to monitor your rate of speaking. When I give a presentation for the first time, I often write "Slow Down" on the top of each note card.

Above all, make sure you know your subject. Again, practice your talk at least two or three times before you deliver it formally. Try giving it without your notes. Anticipate questions and weaknesses in what you are reporting. And remember, in just a few minutes, it will all be over. One way I reduce anxiety is to have the courage of my convictions—I believe in what I have to say and that I am worth a listen!

2. *Flexibility.* Although you should know the major points you will raise in your presentation, try to adapt your delivery to the audience's reaction. Watch what they are doing as you speak. Look directly at the faces of audience members. Do they nod approvingly at an observation you just made? (Elaborate on this point.) Do they look confused? (Clarify your point, or ask for a question.) Do they appear to be falling asleep? (Consider cutting short your discussion of the point.) Fine-tuning your presentation in ways such as these requires that you know your material well. Being able to include additional examples or clarification that can be evoked in an emergency will help you make these transitions if you are not comfortable relying on your extemporaneous abilities.

3. *Clarity.* Emphasize the organization of your talk by giving clear verbal signposts of each major point. Change your tone of voice, pause, or speak more slowly; gestures can serve as visual punctuation marks. Make sure your listeners know exactly where you are in your presentation at any given moment. Begin by giving a direct, summary statement of your conclusion, and follow it with an outline of the issues you will discuss to support this conclusion.

About two thirds of the way through, it may be appropriate to say something like, "I want to devote most of the remaining few minutes to. . . ." As you near the end of your talk, let your audience know you are about to end—for example, by saying, "In closing, I would like to make two broad observations about these data." Avoid confusing transitions in the middle of your presentation, such as "finally," "one last point," and "to conclude"; your audience may wonder why you are continuing to speak. One method I use to ensure clarity is to ask my audience, usually students, to decide on the most confusing point I have made, which I then clarify at the end of class.

4. *Answering questions.* If you have done a thorough job of preparing your talk, you will have some idea of what kinds of questions people are likely to ask. Even if you are caught by surprise, you will probably be able to provide a reasonable answer to someone's question. You have been working with your subject for quite a while by now, and that makes you somewhat of an expert. Try to organize your answer to the question as the person is asking it. Keep your answer as brief as possible; don't use the question-and-answer period as an opportunity to give another presentation. If the question is at all complex, repeat or rephrase it for the benefit of your audience, and then go on to answer it. If you don't fully understand a question, ask the person to rephrase it, or try to rephrase it yourself and ask the person if you have interpreted it correctly. If you don't know the answer to a question, say so. You might then ask the questioner how he or she might respond; for example, "That's a very interesting idea I hadn't considered. What do you think its implications are for. . . ?" Finally, attempt to answer questions from a representative number in the audience, as a few self-important members may wish to monopolize your time.

ESSAY EXAMINATIONS

Few students like to take examinations. At least some of this distaste for examinations is related to a misperception of their nature and purpose. Professors are seldom looking for profound, original insights in answers to examination questions. Even though you may have studied for days, the conditions under which exams are administered usually preclude deeply thoughtful answers. What instructors are looking for is an honest attempt to answer the question, a logical and well-organized answer, and an answer that indicates you have read, understood, and are able to identify major themes in course materials. They want to know that you understand the reading and class notes, not simply that you can give them back on an examination.

Preparing for Examinations

Probably your experience has already indicated that you may learn more studying for the final examination than at any other point in the course. Even if your performance on the examination was not all you had hoped for, preparing for the examination forced you to summarize the major themes of the course, to make connections among what might have appeared as a dozen minicourses during the term, and to confront your understanding (or lack of understanding) of the course materials directly. The following are nothing more than a set of study hints that will help you get more out of preparing for an exam.

1. Attempt to read everything that has been assigned for the course, and prepare summaries of each article or book. Ask yourself, "Why was this book assigned for the course? What general issue does this article address? How was this book or article incorporated into class discussions or lectures?" Try to associate the authors of the assigned readings with major concepts discussed in their work (e.g., Robert Merton—"self-fulfilling prophecy," Emile Durkheim—"anomie," and Erving Goffman—"total institutions"). Both in undergraduate and graduate work, discussion groups using shared outlines can contribute to a better general understanding of voluminous readings. Hopefully, each member will help others grasp points that they may have missed in their own study. Finally, textbooks often have

discussion questions that can help you identify what might be asked; some even have web exercises and online discussion groups.

2. After you summarize each article or book, think of additional examples that support (or fail to support) the conclusions of the author. Illustrations of your own will demonstrate your general understanding of the issues raised in the context of particular studies. The idea is to demonstrate that you actively think about what you read; professors pray for evidence of analysis and reflection, rather than mind-numbing recapitulation in test after test.

3. Search for connections between course materials. Which studies can be logically grouped together? Which studies offer conflicting perspectives or conclusions? If you look for patterns in the readings before the exam, questions that ask you to compare or contrast two perspectives or authors will be easier to answer.

4. Analyze the course. Examinations are not a test of everything you have covered in a course; they consist of a sample of questions drawn from a broad range of topics. Consequently, you should not be angry with your instructor if you end up studying a lot of material that is not included in the examination. Instead, critically analyze the course to determine what topics are likely to appear on the examination. Which topics were emphasized in the course? Did the instructor focus primarily on theoretical, empirical, or methodological themes in course materials? What did you talk about in class discussions? I'm not suggesting that you draw your own sample of course materials and then study only these. Taking that kind of Las Vegas gamble can easily backfire. On the other hand, you should not study indiscriminately. Needless to say, methodical note taking of readings and lectures *when assigned* will enable you to realistically review the semester's work. Finally, outline or even write out essay answers at home, under timed conditions, if you have been given potential questions to prepare.

Taking the Examination

Although these remarks assume that you are taking an examination with prescribed time limits, they should also assist you in writing a take-home examination. I have had some excellent students who failed to understand the hard rules of essay exams, even though they had faithfully read the texts and did well in class. Here are the basics.

1. Read through the entire examination before writing anything. If someone is proctoring the exam, ask for clarification of any question you do not fully understand. If you have a choice of which questions to answer, tentatively identify the ones you will complete. I say "tentatively" because later, having answered "A," you may get good ideas for "C," and so go on to answer "C" instead of (as you first thought) "B." That is, while answering one question, you might get ideas for another. (Or, indeed, you may realize that you *don't* have any ideas for a question you intended to answer.) Obtaining an overview of the examination helps settle your nerves, assuming you have not made the major mistake of staying up all night fearfully cramming.

2. Answer the easiest questions first. You should be able to get through these quickly, leaving time for questions you find more difficult. If you are writing in an examination book, don't feel obliged to answer the questions in the order in which they appear on the exam; you will unknowingly be working on the ones you leave for later. You should, however, follow the general framework set forth in the examination. If, for example, you are asked to define five terms and write three short essays, don't intersperse a few definitions between each essay. Instead, allow enough room so that you can place all of the definitions together, even if you do not write them all at once. And be sure to identify, by number or letter, the questions you are answering. Often it is useful to rephrase the question at the beginning of your answer, for example,

QUESTION: Using a conflict perspective, critically evaluate functional theories of social change.
ANSWER: "Conflict theorists reject functional explanations of social change on four grounds. First,..." [Clear to both you and your instructor.]

3. Pay attention to the weight accorded different questions. If some questions are weighted more heavily in the calculation of the examination grade, spend more time (and write more) on these. Avoid the temptation to write too much about an easy question only to treat superficially another, more significant one. No matter how well some answers are written, they cannot atone for the ones omitted for lack of planning.

4. Read each question carefully. If the question says to "compare," then discuss similarities and dissimilarities among the subjects of the question. If it says "list," then name and describe the appropriate items. (Examples of each item are often welcome additions to lists.) If the question asks for your opinion about something, then give it and substantiate your answer with evidence; otherwise, refrain from casual remarks preceded by "I think . . ." or "I believe. . . ."

It is my impression that when students try to answer questions that baffle them, they often rely on the shotgun approach. Practitioners of this method begin by identifying several key words in the question. They then proceed to write as much as they know about each key word, with little regard for the specific focus of the question. Consider, for example, the following question:

> We have discussed four perspectives of deviant behavior, yet it is not clear that they are equally powerful explanations for a given form of deviance. Do some theories seem to be appropriate explanations for only some types of deviance? Under what conditions is one perspective more useful than another?

Students applying the shotgun approach to this question would immediately begin to write down everything they can remember about each of the theories of deviance discussed in the course. Although some degree of background information concerning these theories is necessary to answer the question, an indiscriminate attempt to summarize several weeks of class materials rather than critically evaluate does nothing more than waste valuable time that might be spent answering other questions. You cannot expect to get full credit for your essay without answering the substance, the point of the question. (In my example, this comes in the last sentence of the question.)

5. Take a few minutes to prepare a brief outline of each question on the inside cover of your exam book before writing your essay. An outline focuses and organizes your answer, and once it is done, you have gone more than halfway toward answering the question. If the question asks you to "List four characteristics of bureaucracy as defined by Max Weber," your outline should consist of four characteristics with cryptic notes (perhaps illustrations) listed under each. If the questions asks you to "Compare bureaucratic and nonbureaucratic forms of organization," you might construct a table of two columns across the top (one for each type of organization) and rows down the side for each trait on which you will compare these organizations, as shown in Figure 6.1.

6. Despite the pressure of time (you will want to write down everything you know), write as legibly as possible. If most instructors are like me, they relegate the illegible blue books to the bottom of the pile, only to be reopened after mustering a strong resolve to finish grading. In addition to writing as neatly as possible, try other methods to ease the strain on your instructor's eyesight and patience; write on every other line, with a reliable pen rather than

Characteristics	*Bureaucratic*	*Nonbureaucratic*
1. Authority	*hierarchical*	*dispersed/collective*
2. Rules	*formal*	*informal*
3. Division of Labor	*complex*	*simple*
4. Social relations	*impersonal/role-based*	*personal*

■ *Figure 6.1*

pencil, and on only one side of the page. As I mention in the chapter on form, a messy paper may lead your reader to focus on appearance, not content. Also be sure to bring an extra bluebook to allow for complete answers.

7. Don't assume that your instructor will read between the lines of your examination. Although most instructors give students the benefit of the doubt in ambiguous situations, they are forced to mark examinations on the basis of what has been written, not on what might have been written. That is why practicing writing is so important: to prepare you to clearly explain what you mean in different forums, from term papers to essay tests. Instructors will not assume that you knew more about the question and simply ran out of time or that you could have provided a relevant citation or example but chose not to do so. If you do run out of time before finishing a question, you might conclude with a sketchy outline of the rest of your answer. This will at least demonstrate to your instructor that you might have written a more complete answer, given more time.

Sample Examination Answers

Here are two answers to a question that appeared on a final examination in an introductory sociology class The question was, "In what ways does Ralph Turner's description of the origins of significant social movements differ from earlier strain theories?" Answering this question requires writing a comparison. The student must first describe "earlier strain theories" of social movements and then show how Turner's theory differs from these. Structured analysis is the goal rather than an unrelated series of descriptions.

There are several important differences (in addition to length) between these two answers. The first answer—the weaker of the two—moves too quickly to a discussion of Turner's work. Although the author need not offer a definition of social movements, she should provide a more detailed description of strain theories. Similarly, when the author of Answer A turns to a discussion of Turner's work, she does not provide enough detail about his theory of social movements. Her discussion of redefining the situation as injustice rather than misfortune dominates the remainder of the answer, yet different types of social movements are neither described nor illustrated.

ANSWER A

Earlier strain theories stated that whenever the conditions of a certain group of people got bad enough, they would rebel or revolt and try to change and improve their situation. However, this explanation didn't give reasons as to why, when conditions were bad for an extended period of time, people would rebel at one specific time.

Turner's description varied from these earlier theories in that he argued that in addition to bad conditions, it was necessary for the people in this situation to redefine their situation, labeling it as no longer tolerable. Generally, Turner explained that this redefinition would come about after an improvement in the people's situation, at which time they would look back and decide that the conditions that they had accepted all along were, in fact, no longer acceptable.

The question of redefining a situation has to do with how the situation is perceived. A classic example of this would be "misfortune" versus "fate." In the former, the situation is defined as being bad, but the victim doesn't blame anyone or seek reparations. The situation is seen as something that can't be helped, perhaps a consequence of fate. In the latter, the situation is also perceived as being bad, but it is no longer "accepted," in any sense of the word. It is now perceived as someone's (or something's) fault. Here, some sort of reparation or compensation is due the victim.

With these cases, the reaction of the victim varied, depending on how the situation is perceived and defined ("misfortune" or "injustice"). With a misfortune, the victim does not feel necessarily entitled to help or reparation, and as such, his or her only recourse in seeking such assistance would

```
be to beg or plead. When an injustice is done, the
victim feels entitled to such help or reparations,
and as such, feels free to demand it.
```

In addition to the problems I have already mentioned, Answer A is somewhat repetitive. The last paragraph does little more than reiterate the issues presented in the previous paragraph and represents general reaction more than reference to specific authors or theories in the course. Most of us have some idea of the questions that social scientists raise, but this minor knowledge does not substitute our knowledge for theirs.

The second answer, in contrast, begins by defining social movements and summarizing earlier strain theories. It then goes on to describe three previous theories, in each case referring to their authors. After an effective transition at the beginning of the third paragraph, the author provides a fairly detailed discussion of Turner's theory of social movements. She writes about the critical importance of redefining social conditions in the context of three types of social movements described by Turner, offering examples of each type, and concludes by describing the conditions under which these redefinitions occur.

ANSWER B

```
Many social scientists have attempted to explain
social movements, events that occur when people
come together with the intention of bringing about
or resisting cultural, economic, or political
change. Early strain theories assumed that when
enough discontent arises among enough people, the
inevitable result is an outburst of some kind.
Alexis de Tocqueville suggested that a social
movement takes place after a period of strain,
followed by a period of advancement. Once an
oppressed people received a taste of "the good
life," they would no longer be able to suffer
silently. Karl Marx argued that when the peasants
became so pauperized, starving, and poor that they
could no longer stand it, they would initiate the
Communist Revolution. Building on these theories,
```

James Davis, a contemporary social scientist, claimed that a social movement is likely to occur after a period of advancement, followed by a period of stagnation. Employing the notion of "increasing expectancies," he argued that people would continue to expect more and that when it never came, they would join together in a social movement.

None of these strain explanations accounts for the fact that social conditions are bad for some people all of the time. Taking Marx's example, the question could be asked: "Why didn't the peasants, who had been suffering for centuries, rebel sooner?"

Ralph Turner's description of the origins of significant social movements supplies the answer to this question. Turner felt that strain was not enough: Oppressed groups must redefine their situation. Where they once saw their conditions as misfortune—as a fate which they could do little to change—they come to see the same condition as an injustice, brought about by others. When the condition is defined as an injustice, the frequent response is revolt.

Turner distinguished three types of social movements and the redefinition necessary for them to occur. In a liberal humanitarian movement, such as the French Revolution, people come to see their inability to participate in politics as an injustice. In social reform movements, such as the Communist Revolution, people redefine their lack of material wealth as an injustice. Finally, in contemporary social movements, such as the Women's Liberation Movement, the denial of personal fulfillment is no longer seen as an unavoidable misfortune but as a curable injustice.

Turner's theory, after answering the question of why revolt takes place when it does, goes on to explain why the redefinition of social conditions occurs. According to Turner, people redefine their condition when there is a rise in the conditions of the major class without a corresponding increase in other social statuses. This inconsistency propels

```
them to act. In a liberal humanitarian movement, a
rise in economic wealth, but a lack of political
power, can be viewed as the motivating
inconsistency. In social reform movements, greater
numbers acquiring jobs but not job security can be
seen as a cause. The inconsistency that promotes a
contemporary reform movement is a rise in personal
autonomy, but a social inhibition to exercise this
independence.
```

Although both of these answers make the same general point, the second answer is more thorough and informative. Providing clear definitions and using well-chosen examples, the author of the second answer has written a significantly stronger essay.

QUESTIONS ON PRESENTATIONS AND EXAMINATIONS

1. Why do oral presentations require so much careful planning and practice?

2. How can you reduce anxiety before speaking? For example, do you know your audience?

3 Have you rehearsed your speech several times beforehand, in front of a helpful listener?

4. Do you write your speech in such a way to avoid reading it directly to your audience?

5. Do you time your speech to allow for questions to connect you more fully to the group?

6. Do you understand that instructors want articulate reflection on written examinations?

7 Do you understand how following simple but essential rules on tests can conserve time?

8. Have you reviewed old tests to review mistakes, such as generality or lack of organization?

FORM

■ ■ ■

Form refers to what your paper looks like: Is it typed double-spaced? Are the margins adequate? Are the quotation marks in the right place? Are sources properly acknowledged? Did you use the required citation style for the discipline, publication, or your demanding professor? Following proper form does more than make your paper look nice. It makes a difference in how others read your work; a messy or carelessly referenced paper distracts readers from the point you are trying to make. Failing to follow proper form may even determine whether your paper is read at all. Many journals return manuscripts to authors who do not meticulously follow the guidelines for submissions, and instructors may refuse to accept papers that they judge too flawed to read. More important, form can affect the content of your writing Misplaced quotation marks or failure to acknowledge sources can result in plagiarism, a problem often caused by haste but nonetheless inexcusable.

The accepted forms in sociology, psychology, and political science, for example, differ from each other; even within any *one* of these disciplines, forms often differ among journals. The material in this chapter outlines essential advice on questions of form that arise in social science writing and explains the logic behind some major form types. You will still need to periodically consult the official style manual in each discipline, especially for complex questions, such as how to cite a quote imbedded in another quote in a secondary source. These highly detailed texts, such as the *Chicago*

Manual of Style, are revised periodically and may be found in the reference section of the library, at your university writing center, and on the Internet.

Regardless of whether you follow this or another set of guidelines, the important thing about manuscript form is *consistency*. Make certain that citations of works by a single author follow the same pattern, that footnotes are consistent in style, and so forth. Consistency of form will help your reader focus on what you have written, not on how it appears on the page. Software programs are now available to help ensure absolute consistency in each type of form, which substantially reduce the chances of unintended mistakes and speeds up a once laborious process for students and scholars. These ever more powerful systems will automatically format citations, for example, and construct and organize a bibliography in any required style as you construct the document, which is particularly useful for larger studies.

MANUSCRIPT FORM

Most people assume they know how to put a paper together before they hand it in. At the risk of insulting your intelligence, and in the *absence* of contrary specifications from an instructor, here are some guidelines for preparing the final draft of a manuscript:

1. Type or print your manuscript on 8½ by 11-inch paper. Use conventional typing paper; avoid the variety of exotic papers—onion skin, colored, lined, scented, spiral-bound, bordered, or whatnot—found on the shelves of campus bookstores. If you type your paper on a word processor and print it on continuous-feed paper, remove the perforated edges, separate the pages, and arrange them in correct order. Laser printers now make the cleanest, fastest copies and can use quality paper, qualities often required by journal editors and easier on your instructor's overworked eyes. For those who complete assignments at the last minute, be aware that university owned printers used by students often break down at crucial times in the semester.

2. Type, double-spacing, on one side of the paper only. Make sure the ink on your final copy is dark enough to be read easily. Avoid fonts that are too large or small.

3. If your paper is fairly long (10 pages or more), include a title page. Center your title about midway down the page. Roughly 1 inch from the bottom, center your name, the course number or name, and the date. If the title is longer than one line, double-space it. Single-space the information about authorship.

If you do not use a title page, place your name, course title, and date in the upper right-hand corner of the page (single-spaced), about 1 inch from the top. Skip two lines and center your title, double-spacing between lines for long titles. Leave three or four lines before starting your paper.

4. Capitalize the first and last words of your title, as well as all other words except articles, conjunctions, and prepositions. Do not place the title in quotation marks or underline it. If, however, the title contains the name of a book, the book title should be underlined; for example,

```
An Analysis of the Loss of Community in Erikson's
Everything in Its Path
```

5. Provide ample and uniform margins for your paper. Allow 1½ inches for the left margin and 1 inch for the right, bottom, and top margins. Annotations are easier to make and to read with generous margins. At the opposite extreme, do not "pad" your paper with outsized margins or fonts.

6. Number pages consecutively. If you use a title page, don't number it. The first page of your paper need not be numbered either, but number each subsequent page (beginning with 2) in the same place, either in the upper right-hand corner or centered at the bottom of the page. Do *not* put a period after the number. Place your last name in the upper right-hand corner of each page, and skip two lines before beginning the text. Pages with notes and references should be numbered as text, but you need not number pages with tables or appendices attached to the end of the paper.

7. Indent a uniform number of spaces—either five or eight—at the beginning of each paragraph. Direct quotations longer than four lines should be indented (also five or eight spaces) and typed single-spaced (see the next section, on "Quotations and Quotation Marks").

8. Make a paper and a computer file copy of your paper before handing it in. Your instructor probably shares your fear of losing a paper and may have lost a few! Fires, burglaries, and other acts of fate have claimed entire dissertations, so always keep multiple copies of major papers in separate locations.

9. Staple your paper in the upper left-hand corner; paper clips can become attached to other student papers. If your paper is too long for a standard staple, use some sort of heavy clip to hold it together. Avoid those clear plastic binders that can cause an avalanche of student papers on an instructor's desk. And avoid stiff folders that add bulk to an instructor's load.

QUOTATIONS AND QUOTATION MARKS

Both quotations and quotation marks are powerful writing devices when used sparingly. They signal your reader to pay close attention to what is being said. When overused, however, they can have the opposite effect, prompting your reader to skim through the quoted material in search of the point you are trying to make. You are *writing* a paper, not compiling an anthology. For each quotation you consider including in your paper, ask the following questions:

Can I write a valid and concise summary or paraphrase of these words? If you can accurately convey the meaning of the quoted material, you should probably summarize or paraphrase it and properly acknowledge the source (see the next section, on citation form). A *summary* is a condensation of the original, a *paraphrase* (putting it in your own words) can be as long as the original or even longer. You don't want to swamp your paper with long quotations, so, for balance, you summarize. Papers composed of an endless stream of direct quotations not only are boring to read, but they fail to demonstrate an understanding of the source materials themselves. You also don't want to jar your reader by even a short quotation of someone else's distinctive voice (unless it is that distinctive voice you want to emphasize), so you paraphrase.

Sometimes a summary won't do: It would take more words or an awkward construction to capture the essence of the quotation (e.g., the author's choice of words cannot be improved on), or the quotation is to be used as a primary source for a point you will make (e.g., interviews from a field study or a quotation from a political figure). In these cases don't hesitate to quote directly. Just be sure to keep track of the balance in your paper between your own words and the words of others. Caution: When you summarize or paraphrase, be sure to give credit to your source, even if you are putting the material entirely into your own words. Lastly, "patchwork plagiarism" occurs when you accidentally use phrases or sentences from the original source mixed with your own; this problem usually arises when you've waited until the last minute to write your paper. Students often commit this sin unintentionally, and the only reliable cure is a foolproof system of note-taking and enough lead time to allow for the question, "are these my words"?

Do I need this quotation to make my point, and do I adequately explain why I am using this quotation? Make certain that you, as well as your readers, know why each quotation appears in your paper. After conducting sustained research, the reason for using a quote is abundantly evident to you but not necessarily to your reader. The simplest way to explain its inclusion is to introduce and follow the quotation with some discussion of it. The language you use to introduce the quoted material should do more than state the source; it should convey a sense of your purpose in including the material in your paper. Instead of writing, "Goffman says, . . . ," you might write, "Goffman claims, . . ." or "Goffman, on the other hand, concludes, . . ." or even "With customary eloquence, Goffman analyzes the dilemma that accompanies a shift in virtual and actual identities: . . . ." Instead of writing, "Two respondents said: . . . ," you might write, "Placed side-by-side, the remarks of these two respondents illustrate the differences in motivation among group members: . . . ." Your discussion of quoted material, as well as the material itself, should be purposive rather than declaratory, analytic rather than descriptive.

Is this a special case? Quotation marks are sometimes used to call attention to a concept or phrase of particular attribution. Many social science concepts are associated with their creators: Toennies's "Gemeinschaft" and "Gesellschaft," Cooley's "looking-glass self," Gans's "urban villagers," and Reisman's "other-directedness" come to mind. When we enclose these words in quotation marks, we are telling our readers that we have borrowed them, and we intend them to have the meaning given them by their originators. Because your paper can easily become cluttered with quotation marks, you might consider placing quotation marks only around the first occurrence (or underlining it) and omitting further identifying marks from later references to the phrase. If there is any doubt as to the meaning of such terms, define them for your intended audience or instructor.

Once you decide which quotations to include in your paper, use the appropriate form to incorporate them. These rules can serve as basic guidelines:

1. Always identify the source of the quotation. Your reader should never have to guess who or what the source of quoted material was. If you are quoting library materials, cite the author, year of publication, and page on which the material appears—for instance (Jones 1985:227), (Bureau of the Census 1981). (See the following section, "Citations Within the Text.") If you are quoting interviews you have conducted, give appropriate identifying information in parentheses after the quotation—for example, "(female, 42 years old, office manager)."

2. Distinguish between short and long quotations. If a quotation is four typewritten lines or less, incorporate it (double-spaced) into the text, using quotation marks. For example,

> In commenting on the role of secrecy in
> bureaucracy, Weber observes that "bureaucratic
> administration always tends to be an administration

of 'secret sessions': insofar as it can, it hides
its knowledge and action from criticism" (Gerth and
Mills 1976:233).

Quotations longer than four typewritten lines should be indented, single-spaced, and set off from the text by two blank lines. Do not place quotation marks around the material that is thus set off.

The tendency toward secrecy in certain
administrative fields follows their material
nature: everywhere that the power interests of the
domination structure toward <u>the outside</u> are at
stake, whether it is an economic competitor of a
private enterprise, or a foreign, potentially
hostile polity, we find secrecy (Gerth and Mills
1976:233).

3. *Quote materials exactly.* Anything placed within quotation marks should be the exact words found in the source. Do not alter verb tense, subject–verb agreement, or anything else about the quotation to make it fit into your text. Instead, change your text to conform to the quotation.

Similarly, retain the original punctuation and emphasis when quoting materials. In the first quotation from Weber, the phrase "secret sessions" appears in quotation marks in the source. Thus, the quotation marks are retained in the text, but as single, rather than double, quotes. (Single quotation marks are normally used for quotes within a quote.) In the second quotation, because the phrase "the outside" appears in italics in the original text, it is underlined in the quotation. If this phrase had not been emphasized in the source, but I wanted to draw attention to it myself, I would have appended the words "emphasis mine" to the citation (e.g., "Gerth and Mills 1976:233, emphasis mine"). To ensure absolute accuracy in a quote, either photocopy the original or print it from an online source.

Sometimes quoted material contains mistakes of one kind or another: an awkward phrase or construction, or a factual error. Such mistakes are common in direct transcriptions of interviews, where respondents may say one thing early in the interview and later contradict themselves. In such cases, attribute the odd phrase, expression, or outmoded spelling in the original source by placing the word "*sic*" after it in parentheses. This way your reader won't think your paper contains a misprint or typographical error. For instance, you may use a quotation in which a respondent says that he moved to Boston in 1977. In another quotation you want to include from the same interview, this man says "In 1979 (*sic*), when we first came to Boston . . . ," you note the change of date by placing *sic* immediately after 1979.

Finally, if you must alter the original quotation to include it properly in the text, identify any words you *add* by placing them in brackets, not parentheses, inside of the quotation marks; indicate *omission* of any words by ellipses (three periods, with a letter-space between each of the periods). While researching a book on Alaska, I came across the following text from a report issued by the Alaska Statehood Commission:

> The overwhelming majority of Alaskans, including all members of this commission, consider themselves Americans. We remember with deep gratitude the spring of 1964, when money and equipment and manpower came from across America to rebuild our earthquake crumpled coastal cities. That support drew on vast stores of supplies and equipment that an independent Alaska could never provide. We are proud to be citizens of a nation which responded so generously, and want to pass this citizenship to our descendants. (Alaska Statehood Commission 1982:40)

To shorten the quotation yet preserve its meaning, I arrived at this revision (note that the ellipsis is followed by a fourth period because it ends a sentence):

> The overwhelming majority of Alaskans, including all members of this commission, consider themselves

Americans. . . . We are proud to be citizens of a
nation which responded so generously [to the
devastation wrought by the earthquake of 1964], and
want to pass this citizenship to our descendants.
(Alaska Statehood Commission 1982:40)

CITATIONS WITHIN THE TEXT

Since the last publication of this book, there has been increased
standardization of citation styles in the social sciences. The
American Sociology Association and American Political Science
Association use the ASA and APSA systems respectively, both based
on the *Chicago Manual of Style* (CMS). The American Psychological
Association uses its own system (APA), which is also used in fields
such as education and nursing. Journals in most social science fields
may specify their own preferred forms, although they are usually
similar to the major ones listed above. Professors may even prefer
citation formats that are not their discipline's standard. The rules
outlined in this section illustrate some fundamental guidelines for
placing citations within the text. Check with your instructor (or a
specific journal's style sheet) to make sure you choose the appropriate form. University libraries usually have the latest copy of the
major style manuals and can direct you to electronic sources of advice for questions not yet addressed in the printed volume. For
example, the latest citation requirements and other research advice
often appear on the web sites of social science professional organizations or major journals. This instant access is particularly important
when citing electronic information because of the evolving nature of
citation requirements from this medium.

For most social science papers, citations of source material,
regardless of whether you paraphrase or quote directly, are made
within the text, not within footnotes. The citations provide enough
information so that your reader can find the complete reference for
the source material at the end of your paper, in the references or bibliography section, without the distraction of footnotes or endnotes

interrupting the reader. Attempt to understand the general reason of the following advice, even if you forget more specific rules, such as comma placement, in the format in question. The specific form of text citations varies slightly, depending on what is being cited, but the following general rules apply to all text citations:

1. When the author's name is not mentioned in the text of your paper, it should be included in the citation, along with the date of publication, and sometimes the page number. All of this information is placed in parentheses directly after the cited material; the author's name is followed by a space, and using the ASA system, the date of publication is followed by a colon when a page number is included. (If you are following APA or APSA style guidelines, you would place a comma between the author's name and the date of publication.) Page numbers should be given when you feel that they would be helpful to the reader; they are always used when the cited material is quoted directly.

```
The image of the frontier evolved out of the
"paired but contradictory ideas of nature and
civilization" (Smith 1954:305). These results
support the information hypothesis (Ritchey 1976),
which argues that migrants learn of economic
opportunities from established residents.
```

Notice that the authors, Smith in the first example and Ritchey in the second, are named within the parenthetical citation because they are not named in the paper's text. Notice, as well, that the citation is placed outside of the quotation marks, and the period that ends the sentence appears *after* the closing parenthesis.

2. When an author is mentioned in the text, the name is not repeated in the citation, but the date (and if directly quoted, the page number) is given in parentheses after the author's name.

```
Hans Morgenthau (1965, 328) considered massive
retaliation, " . . . an invitation to Armageddon."
[APSA system]
```

3. When repeated citations to the same reference are made, give the date and page number (if appropriate) for the first citation; for later citations, list only the page number. This rule is appropriate when the subject of your paper is a detailed analysis of one or two texts. Because it should be obvious to the reader that you are repeatedly quoting the same source, the date of publication is superfluous.

> The assumptions implicit in Karl Marx's later writing are found in his Economic and Philosophical Manuscripts of 1844 (1961). It is there, for example, that we find the clearest outline of his conceptions regarding human nature, Marx (36) writes:. . . .

If, however, you make repeated references to several works by one author, you must provide complete citations (including both year of publication and page number) for each work, following the form described in Rules 1 and 2.

4. For serial citations (i.e., when several sources provide evidence for the same argument), list the authors in alphabetical order, and separate the citations with semicolons. Enclose the multiple citations in parentheses.

> Friends and family members may encourage migration by providing information about economic opportunities or social conditions elsewhere (Bieder 1973; Brown et al. 1963; Choldin 1973; Litwak 1960).

5. When a source has two authors, include both last names in the citation. When a source has three or more authors, list all last names on the first citation in the text; thereafter, follow the first author's name with et al. (the Latin abbreviation for *et alii*, meaning "and other people"). The references section, however, includes the last names of all authors for a given source. The examples in Rules 2 and 4 illustrate how to cite works of joint authorship.

6. When you include two or more works written by the same person in the same year, designate them "a," "b," and so forth. Usually, citations are labeled in the order in which they appear in the text, for example, the first appearance is "a," the second is "b."

```
Gove (1970a, b) has been one of the most outspoken
critics of labelling theory.
```

7. When two or more authors have the same last name, identify each in the text by the appropriate initials.

```
Evidence that both confirms (R. J. Smith 1983) and
disputes (J. K. Smith 1984) this hypothesis has
been uncovered.
```

8. When citing unpublished materials, use "forthcoming" if the material is scheduled for publication. Cite the date for dissertations and other unpublished papers. If the material you are citing is not dated, place "(n.d.)" after the author's name.

```
In a recent article Hummon (forthcoming) summarizes
the interdisciplinary literature on place identity.
```

9. When the source is a machine-readable data file, note the producer of the file and the date of production.

```
The data used in this paper are from the General
Social Survey (Institute for Social Research 1993).
```

10. When citing electronic sources, it is best to consult the latest approved form available on the Internet, either on the web sites of style manuals, major journals, or advice organizations linked to these sites. Librarians usually have lists of these advice sites, which are often operated by major research universities. The continual debate on exactly how to cite from this medium has resulted in evolving rules, both in the parent citation systems such as the CMS and

the derived ones used in disciplines like sociology. The APA system, for example, requires author and date, and page number if citing a quotation, in an in-text citation. Be aware that required information, such as page number of the document, required by the MLA for example, is not always available.

THE LIST OF WORKS CITED

The references section of your paper elaborates on the text citations by giving the complete names of authors, places of publication, publishers, and page numbers. Every text citation must be included in the references; any materials not cited in the text are usually omitted from the references. The format for entries is determined by the type of research material. The Internet has variations in sources as well, such as electronic journals or online books.

Bibliographic form varies from discipline to discipline, and the examples shown here follow the currently accepted guidelines of the American Sociological Association. In most cases, this form parallels that followed by the APA, with the following notable differences: (1) only the initials of the author's first and middle names are used in APA bibliographies; (2) the date of publication is enclosed in parentheses in APA bibliographies; and (3) for multiple citations by a single author, APA guidelines suggest listing the author each time and arranging the citations by year of publication. The logic of the examples below is similar for all major social science citation systems, with minor variations for each type.

Fortunately, the standardization of bibliographical form is becoming less problematic for those who use computers for word processing. As previously noted, computer software is now available that allows you to enter the elements of each citation (e.g., author, title, date of publication) into a file. When you are ready to produce a list of references, you simply select a publishing style—such as APA or American Political Science Association—and the software produces a bibliography formatted in the selected style. You can also switch formats to fit differing requirements, for example APA to CMS, which is useful as form types are revised periodically or have variations required by journals.

Books with a Single Author

References to books include the author's name (last name first), the date of publication, the title of the book, the place of publication, and the publisher (in this order).

```
Williams, Patricia J. 1991. The Alchemy of Race and
     Rights. Cambridge, MA: Harvard University Press.
```

The author's last name, flush against the left margin, is followed by a comma, the first name, and a period. (If a middle initial is used, a second period is not appended.) A period is also placed after the date of publication. The title, underlined continuously, ends with a period. Subtitles are commonly omitted from the references (unless APA style is being followed). The place of publication is given by town or city name and abbreviated state name, separated by a comma. Place of publication is followed by a colon and ends with the name of the publisher. Note that the second (and any additional) line in the reference is indented. The references should also be typed double-spaced.

Books with More Than One Author

If a book has two authors, list it alphabetically by the last name of the first author. The second author's name is listed in normal order—first name first.

```
Powell, Woody and Paul DiMaggio. 1991. The New
     Institutionalism in Organizational Analysis.
     Chicago, IL: University of Chicago Press.
```

If a book has more than two authors, list it alphabetically by the last name of the first author; list the names of all of the remaining authors in normal order as they appear on the title page.

Singleton, Royce A., Jr., Bruce C. Straits, and
    Margaret Miller Straits. 1993. <u>Approaches to Social
    Research</u>. New York, NY: Oxford University Press.

Government Documents

Unless an author appears on the report, list the government agency as the author of the document.

U.S. Bureau of the Census. 1991. <u>Statistical Abstract
    of the United States, 1991</u>. Washington, DC: U.S.
    Government Printing Office.

Works of Corporate Authorship

Sometimes cities, consulting firms, research agencies, or other corporate bodies issue reports on which no author is named. If no publisher is named, assume that the corporate body is the publisher.

Institute for Scientific Information. 1972–1991. <u>SSCI:
    Social Sciences Citation Index</u>. Philadelphia, PA:
    Institute for Scientific Information.

An Edited Book

If you cite a book with an editor but no author (e.g., an edited collection of papers written by others), begin the citation with the editor's last name.

Calhoun, Craig, ed. 1994. <u>Social Theory and the
    Politics of Identity</u>. Cambridge, MA: Blackwell
    Publishers.

A Translated Book

Unless you are discussing the translation itself—for instance, comparing one translation of a work with another—list the book by its author, not by its translator.

```
Khazanov, A. M. 1984. Nomads and the Outside World.
     Translated by Julia Crookenden. New York, NY:
     Cambridge University Press.
```

An Article in an Edited Collection

If you cite a single article in an edited volume of several articles, list the work by the author of the article, not the editor.

```
Heimer, Carol A. 1992. "Doing Your Job and Helping Your
     Friends: Universalistic Norms About Obligations to
     Particular Others in Networks. Pp. 143-164 in
     Organizations and Networks: Structure, Form, and
     Action, edited by N. Nhoria and R. G. Eccles.
     Boston, MA: Harvard Business School Press.
```

An Article in a Scholarly Journal

Place the title of the article in quotation marks; underline the title of the journal. Do not abbreviate either title. Give the volume and page numbers, separated by a colon, at the end of the entry.

```
Adler, Patricia A. and Peter Adler. 1996. "Parent-as-
     Researcher: The Politics of Researching in the
     Personal Life." Qualitative Sociology 19:35-58.
```

An Article in a Popular Magazine

List the article by the author's last name; if no author is given for the article, list it by the title of the article, or by the second word if the first word is "A," "An," or "The." Thus, an anonymous article called "The

American Way of Life" would be listed alphabetically under "American," even though the citation would retain the "The" of the title.

Garland, Susan. 1991. "Throwing Stones at the
    Glass Ceiling." <u>Business Week</u>, August 19, p. 27.
"The Making of a Superstar." 1993. <u>Newsweek</u>,
    March 20, pp. 23-25.

An Article in a Newspaper

The only difference between references for a magazine and those in a newspaper is the inclusion of a section number with a newspaper reference. If the newspaper is not divided into sections, the format is exactly the same.

Martinson, Jacob. 1994. "The Psychology of
    Selflessness." <u>The New York Times</u>, April 15,
    sec. 3:5-6.

Unpublished Work

If a work is scheduled for publication, substitute the word "Forthcoming" for the date of publication, omitting any references to volume or page numbers. For dissertations and other unpublished papers, cite the date (and location of a paper publically presented). If no date for the cited work is known, use "N.d." in place of the date. (Be sure to consult the guidelines for the specific style you are using, as some style sheets recommend that unpublished work not yet accepted for publication be excluded from citation in a manuscript.)

Ross, Catherine E. and John Mirowsky. Forthcoming.
    "Does Employment Affect Health?" <u>Journal of Health
    and Social Behavior</u>.

Machine-Readable Data Files

Begin the citation of a machine-readable data file with the person or persons responsible for collecting the data; if no individuals are identified with the data collection, cite the institutional producer of the file. Following the title of the data file, type "[MRDF]," an abbreviation for machine-readable data file. In place of the publisher, give the name of the distributor of the file.

```
Miller, Warren, Arthur Miller, and Gerald Klein. 1975.
     The CPS 1974 American National Election Study
     [MRDF]. Ann Arbor: Center for Political Studies,
     University of Michigan [producer]. Ann Arbor:
     Inter-University Consortium [distributor].
American Institute of Public Opinion. 1976. Gallup
     Public Opinion Poll #965 [MRDF]. Princeton, NJ:
     American Institute of Public Opinion [producer].
     New Haven, CT: Roper Public Opinion Research
     Center, Yale University [distributor].
```

Multiple Citations for a Single Author

If you cite several works written by the same person, arrange them alphabetically by title, and precede the second and all subsequent entries with eight underlined spaces and a period.

```
Ewick, Patricia. 1994. "Integrating Feminist
     Epistemologies in Undergraduate Research Methods
     Courses." Gender and Society 8:92-105.
——. 1992. "Postmodern Melancholia." Law and Society
     Review 26:755-764.
```

Electronic References

Again, it is vital to check the latest form for references on the web, but two general points might be made: be sure to copy the Uniform Resource Locator (URL) exactly so that others may check your references and be aware that not all information will be available to satisfy each reference format. To return to the evaluation warnings of Chapter 2, the more scholarly electronic sources will have the most complete documentation, such as an online journal based on an established paper copy. There is also significant variety of electronic sources; you may want to cite an e-mail conversation with a political figure, for example.

Combining Entries in a References Section: An Illustration

When you have compiled the relevant information for works to be included in your references section, arrange them alphabetically by the author's last name. Type the entries on a separate page titled "References," double-spacing within and between each entry. Begin the first line of each entry against the left-hand margin, and indent all remaining lines of the entry five to eight spaces. Underline the titles of all books, reports, government documents, journals, magazines, and newspapers.

Here is an illustration of the first page of a references section:

References

Alaska Statehood Commission. 1982. <u>More Perfect Union: A Preliminary Report of the Alaska Statehood Commission</u>. Juneau, AK: Alaska Statehood Commission.

Barnet, Sylvan, and Marcia Stubbs. 1995. <u>Practical Guide to Writing with Additional Readings</u>. New York, NY: HarperCollins.

Becker, Howard S. 1963. <u>Outsiders: Studies in the Sociology of Deviance</u>. New York, NY: Free Press.

———. 1986. <u>Writing for Social Scientists</u>. Chicago, IL: University of Chicago Press.

Cuba, Lee J. 1984. "Reorientations of Self: Residential Identification in Anchorage, Alaska." Pp. 219–237 in <u>Studies in Symbolic Interaction</u>, Vol. 5, edited by Norman K. Denzin. Greenwich, CT: JAI Press.

Gerth, H. H., and C. Wright Mills, eds. 1976. <u>From Max Weber: Essays in Sociology</u>. New York, NY: Oxford University Press.

Homans, George C. 1950. <u>The Human Group</u>. New York, NY:
    Harcourt, Brace and Company.
Hummon, David M. 1986. "Urban Views: Popular
    Perspectives on City Life." <u>Urban Life</u> 15:3–36.

This example contains seven of the first nine entries in the references appearing at the back of this book. In comparing the two bibliographies, note that words italicized in print are underlined in typewritten papers.

NOTES

There is considerable difference of opinion on the utility of notes (footnotes and endnotes) in the social sciences. They are used in history and some political science journals, as well as books in these fields. However in sociology, psychology, and related areas, it is best to follow a simple rule: If possible, avoid them. This rule is based on the assumption that if an idea is important enough to include in a paper, it can (and should) be incorporated into the text. For the professional social scientist, the practice of avoiding notes whenever possible is also encouraged by editors who point to the cost of printing notes. There are, nevertheless, times when notes are an appropriate and important part of social science writing. In general, notes will be necessary only when you are writing long (ten pages or more) social science papers.

Possible Uses of Notes

1. Notes can provide detailed information that would otherwise detract from the narrative flow of the text. A note of this type is often used to elaborate on a research methodology. For example, you might write that "the interview schedule contained several questions designed to measure a respondent's tolerance for residential integration," and append a footnote describing the exact questions

that were asked. If, however, you are planning to attach the interview schedule to the paper as an appendix, you would be better off drawing your reader's attention to this appendix with a parenthetical remark in the text, such as "(see Appendix II)," rather than using a note.

2. Notes can supply additional or analogous examples of a point raised in the text; it can make your point stronger by amplification. Suppose you were writing about how people recognize and respond to strangers in urban neighborhoods. You might focus on how trust is established and maintained in neighborhoods of this sort, but then speculate about the importance of trust in other settings in modern life (e.g., in buyer–seller relationships, in negotiations between corporations, or in author–publisher transactions). If an extended discussion of the importance of trust in modern society is not a major goal of your paper, a footnote might allow you to make this broader point without going too far afield of your thesis. Do not use notes to supply additional citations for an issue raised in the text. Incorporate all of the relevant citations into the text, using the form described earlier in this chapter.

3. Notes can anticipate questions or arguments that your readers might raise. When you write, you make decisions about how to organize your paper, what library materials to include, which tables to include, which explanation to offer for a particular finding, and so forth. Your reader, of course, cannot know how you arrived at all of these decisions, and, at times, you may feel that some sort of explanation is necessary. A note of this type may anticipate and argue against counterarguments (e.g., "You might be thinking that X, rather than Y, accounted for this finding, but let me tell you why that cannot be the case . . . "). Or it might explain why something that might be expected in the text is not there (e.g., "Sex and race were included in previous analyses, but neither of these variables exerted significant, independent effects on the dependent variable."). It can be useful for defining terms if there could be questions in the reader's mind. As with all other notes, use these sparingly. Your paper should not read like a point–counterpoint debate.

The Format for Notes

Two types of notes are commonly used: *footnotes*, which appear at the bottom of the appropriate page of text, and *endnotes*, which are collected and placed at the end of the paper. If you are using a typewriter, endnotes are easier to write, but the variety of text-editing software available makes footnotes equally painless if you are writing on a computer. Understand how your software handles notes; problems can occur when you switch from one edition of a software package to a more modern one. If you use endnotes, type them, double-spaced, on a separate page titled "Notes," and place them immediately after the last page of your text. Paginate the notes as though they were additional pages of text (e.g., if your text ends on page 22, the first page of notes is numbered 23). References (paginated) and appendices and tables (both unpaginated) are placed after the notes.

Both footnotes and endnotes are inserted into the text in the same way. They are numbered consecutively throughout the paper; the numbers (*without* a period) are usually placed at the end of a sentence. The number of the note is either a *superscript* (placed one-half space above the line of text) or enclosed by square brackets immediately following the sentence or phrase being noted.

```
The remainder of our observations yielded
anticipated and consistent results.[1]
The remainder of our observations yielded
anticipated and consistent results. [1]
```

AVOIDING PLAGIARISM

Scholarship is an enterprise founded on trust. Although social science research is designed so that it can be replicated by others, the results of research studies are seldom verified. Because of the time and effort such verification would require, we must assume that both the data *and* their interpretation are the honest work of the author of the research, whether that person is a seasoned scholar or a first-year undergraduate. Without these assumptions, scholarly work would have little value or integrity. That is why the organizations that regulate academic life—universities and professional associations—reserve their harshest penalties for those who fabricate research findings or who appropriate the words and ideas of others. At the student level, plagiarism can be unintentional yet highly dangerous for one's grade, or even continued admittance to the university. Purchasing papers online has become the worst sort of plagiarism for students, but know that professors have access to software and web sites that can identify such "opportunities."

When you present the words or ideas of another as if they were your own, you are plagiarizing. Whether you quote directly or summarize in your own words the ideas of someone else, you must acknowledge your debts. You do so by making proper citations to source materials, following a format such as that described earlier.

As easy as it might seem, claiming the work of others as your own is difficult to get away with. Professors who read student papers or referees who review papers for professional journals are intimately familiar with the published work in their disciplines; acquiring an in-depth knowledge of previous research is a major part of their graduate education. They can usually recognize whether what they are reading has appeared someplace else. But more telling from the standpoint of student papers, professors know what to expect from their students. They do not expect undergraduate students to write papers of the quality published in scholarly journals. Even the use of sophisticated words can reveal an unreported source. Instructor's suspicions are likely to be aroused if they read a paper that appears professional in style or content.

Having been forewarned about the seriousness of plagiarism, how can you make sure no one ever accuses you of it? You can guard against unintentional plagiarism by providing unambiguous citations for either direct quotations or summaries of source materials. An example should help to illustrate. Assume that in the process of researching a paper on societal responses to deviant behavior, you come across the following conclusion by John Kitsuse:

```
In modern society, the differentiation of deviants
from the nondeviant population is increasingly
contingent upon circumstances of situation, place,
social and personal biography, and the
bureaucratically organized activities and agencies
of control. (Kitsuse 1962:256)
```

One way of incorporating this conclusion into your paper is to quote it in its entirety, acknowledging the source as I have done here. Another approach is to retain some of Kitsuse's words, embedded in the context of your own sentence. For example:

```
As a proponent of labelling theory, Kitsuse
(1962:256) argues that who and what is defined as
deviant has more to do with "circumstances of
situation, place, social and personal biography,
and the bureaucratically organized activities and
agencies of control" than with the behavior itself.
```

A third way to use Kitsuse's observation is to paraphrase it using your own words. A good paraphrase does not attempt to follow the same sentence structure or word choice as that of the source material. Instead, it conveys the gist of the original material while presenting the ideas in another voice. An acceptable paraphrase of Kitsuse's material might read something like this (note that because I am not using direct quotation, I have omitted the reference to the page number):

```
Labelling theorists have concluded that who and
what are defined as deviant is determined by a host
of factors that have little to do with behavior
itself—where and when the act is committed, who is
committing it, and who is responding to it (Kitsuse
1962).
```

Compare this with a bad paraphrase of the same material:

```
In contemporary society, distinguishing deviants
from non-deviants is more and more determined by
characteristics of context, location, societal and
individual biography, and the bureaucratic
organization and agencies of social control
(Kitsuse 1962).
```

Here the writer has merely provided synonyms—"contemporary society" for Kitsuse's "modern society," for example. There is no point to this paraphrase. Verbatim quotation of the original sentence is much to be preferred over this mechanical, word-for-word substitution.

In attempting to avoid plagiarism, students sometimes give credit where it is not necessarily due. Some material unearthed by your library research can justifiably be labeled "common knowledge"—information about a topic that requires no citation to a particular source. What qualifies as common knowledge? Anything that is repeatedly mentioned in published materials but never cited is probably fair game—for example, that Spanish is the native language of most immigrants from Cuba. Definitions from standard dictionaries (not specialized dictionaries, such as those mentioned in Chapter 2) do not require acknowledgment, but neither are they likely to add much to your paper. Statements of historical fact (e.g., "The Oneida community was founded in 1848" or "Ronald Reagan began his first term as president in 1980") need not be acknowledged, barring some controversy over the date or location of a particular occurrence. On the other hand, interpretations of historical events must be properly acknowledged (e.g., "When the Oneida community was formed in 1848, a new era in utopian experiments began" or "The election of Ronald Reagan as president in 1980 signaled a dramatic shift in political opinion"). The more you read about a particular subject, the greater the chance you will be able to judge what passes as common knowledge. If in doubt, the obvious solution is to err on the side of caution by acknowledging the source.

AVOIDING SEXIST OR RACIST LANGUAGE

> The leader will not give orders that will not be
> obeyed. . . . If he must give orders when they are
> expected and will be obeyed, he must not give
> orders when they will not and cannot be obeyed.
> The leader must maintain his own position. His
> social rank is in mutual dependence with the
> authority of his orders. When he gives orders that
> are not obeyed, he has by that fact undermined his
> rank and hence the presumption on the part of the
> members of his group that his future orders are to
> be obeyed. Nothing, moreover, will create more
> confusion in the minds of his followers, and
> nothing so quickly lead them to doubt his
> confidence. (Homans 1950:429)

When George Homans published *The Human Group* in 1950, perhaps few readers were put off by the style in which it was written.
Today, however, many would be troubled by the abundance of masculine pronouns in Homans's book. Is he suggesting (in the passage
quoted here) that all leaders are men and, therefore, that the repeated use of masculine pronouns is appropriate? Probably not. But
Homans's style is nevertheless offensive because of its implicit sex-
ism. It would be easy to rewrite this passage without using sexist
language, while retaining its original meaning. In your own writing,
watch out for the unnecessary use of masculine pronouns.

Sexist language creates particular problems in social science
writing, where gender plays a major role in explaining a variety of
social phenomena. To describe leaders, deviants, or managers as
men through the use of masculine pronouns is to imply that either
men occupy the majority of these roles or that men and women
lead, deviate, or manage in the same way. Neither of these scenarios
may be accurate, and the use of sexist language only invites stylistic,
as well as analytical, criticism.

How, then, do you avoid sexist language? Sometimes you can do without personal pronouns—masculine or feminine—altogether. Take, for example, the last sentence of the paragraph quoted previously. One possible revision would be the following:

```
Nothing, moreover, will create more confusion in
the minds of followers, and nothing so quickly move
them to doubt a leader's confidence.
```

In the original, "his" is used to describe "followers," but is this really necessary? To whom other than the leader could the followers belong? I have changed the second "his" to "leader's"; in using the possessive of the role itself, I am able to avoid gender-specific pronouns. (I have also replaced "lead them" with "move them" in order to avoid "lead them to doubt a leader's. . . .") In general, think twice before using personal pronouns in your writing; make sure they are important to what you have to say.

Another way to purge sexist language from your writing is to change "he" to "he and she" (or "she and he") and to replace "his" with "his or her" (or "her or his"). The obvious problem with these substitutions is that they clutter a sentence with tiresome repetitions. A writer can make one or two such replacements without much effect on his or her prose. But he or she may lose the patience of his or her reader if he or she attempts universally to replace "he" with "he or she." (The abbreviated forms "s/he" and "her/his" are not much better.)

The preferred solution is to use, where possible, a plural subject paired with the pronoun "their." To return to Homans, we might rewrite the second sentence of the quotation as follows:

```
If leaders must give orders when orders are
expected and will be obeyed, they must not give
orders when orders will not and cannot be obeyed.
```

Using plurals is the most convenient way of avoiding sexist language. It also does not distort the meaning of statements that are intended to describe social interaction of both women and men.

One final note: Avoid the sexist expressions "man" and "mankind" when referring to attributes or behavior characteristic of all humans. Instead of writing, "It is man's nature to . . . ," write "It is human nature. . . . " Likewise, substitute "humanity" or "people" for "mankind" (e.g., "all of humanity" instead of "all of mankind").

Racist language can be unintentional but highly offensive to the group in question. The old saying that Columbus discovered the New World is both inaccurate and insulting to Native Americans. Another example might state how Belgium developed Central Africa when in fact it ruthlessly exploited the area. Most problems in this area are more subtle and can occur through the use of the passive voice, for example:

```
The Western railroads were built by entrepreneur
Leland Stanford. Thousands of Chinese laborers
built the railroads in the West.
```

QUESTIONS ON FORM

1 Why is following the appropriate form as important as the content of your paper?

2 Did your professor or journal recommend a particular form for papers? Do you know where to find style manuals and advice on the Internet?

3 Have you made a photocopy of your paper and an electronic copy of your work?

4. Have you included only those quotations necessary to support your thesis, introducing and discussing their significance in each instance?

5. Are you confident that the quotations you have chosen are both accurate and cited according to the form style required?

6. Have you investigated the latest way to cite and reference different types of electronic sources?

7. Do you understand why footnotes or endnotes are used in a paper?

8 Have you reviewed for unintentional plagiarism, such as poor paraphrasing or using sentence fragments from your source?

9. Have you checked for sexist or racist terms and understand how to correct them?

REVISING

. . .

In the first chapter, I revised a passage of my own writing. In order to illustrate the process of writing, I discussed the general benefits of rewriting and rethinking, but I didn't take the time to discuss in detail how to revise a paper. In this final chapter, I describe several types of revision—for content, clarity, conciseness, proper word usage, spelling, and grammar—that may help you identify weaknesses in your writing. Thoughtful revision is the key to a professional paper, so return to the manuscript at frequent intervals to inspect and repair your work.

The examples in this chapter, clearly set off for examination, may give the appearance that revising is a simple task; it isn't. Sentences in need of repair do not jump from the page. You must go looking for them or ask others to help you find them. When you read a draft of a paper you have written, bear in mind the importance of objectifying your writing, distancing yourself from your writing, and approaching it as an outsider. (In Chapter 1, I discussed some ways of accomplishing this.) Above all, allow time to put your draft aside, preferably for a day but at least for a few hours, so that you can approach it with a relatively open mind, and allow plenty of time for revision. Editing and rewriting are as much a part of the writing process as committing your initial thoughts to paper.

Although revising requires a substantial investment of time and effort, you don't have to remember a lot of formal grammar or style terms to be a good editor. If you're like most of us, you edit your writing, as Howard Becker (1986) puts it, "by ear." You pause at sentences that don't sound right, and you try to come up with ways of making them sound better. It doesn't matter whether you can't tell a comma fault from a dangling modifier, as long as you make a serious attempt to listen to yourself—that is, to reread the paper with the goal of making it clear and concise. Once you have a basic understanding of common mistakes, you will be able to identify them easily through sustained revision.

Having used my writing as an example in the first chapter, I have chosen samples of writing for this chapter that are not my own. (They are drawn from drafts of papers written by my students and colleagues.) After discussing six types of revision, I end the chapter with a list of questions you should ask yourself as you sit down to edit your paper.

REVISING FOR CONTENT

Does each sentence say something? Every sentence in your paper should make a point; vague and superficial language is sadly common in college papers. Consider the following examples drawn from student papers:

```
Alcoholism is a social problem.

In history people witnessed and practiced
punishment for many centuries, and people today
still exercise it.

Between 1820 and 1860, this country experienced
changes economically, socially, politically, and
territorially.
```

Are you surprised to learn that alcoholism is a social problem, that the history of punishing criminals is long-standing, or that the United States changed in several ways in the 1800s? The emptiness of these sentences is striking. Such statements of the obvious severely weaken a paper; they require a simple editorial response: deletion. Begin from scratch by writing a new sentence that says something.

Vacuous sentences are likely to appear in introductions or conclusions to papers or at the beginning or end of paragraphs. In these places, you may attempt to summarize what you are about to write, or what you have written. In attempting to say too much, you may end up saying nothing. (On the other hand, in *drafting* your paper, don't be afraid to say the obvious. Saying the obvious may help get you going. But when the time comes to revise, take some part of the general idea and make it say something worthwhile).

REVISING FOR CLARITY

Will your imagined readers find your sentences clear? A reader should not have to labor through your paper, stopping to figure out what you had in mind when you wrote a particular sentence. Here are several things to keep in mind as you revise your paper for clarity.

1. *Imprecise wording:* Sometimes clarity is obscured because of poor word choice. Take, for example, the following sentence:

```
There is a distinct relationship between the
socialization and selection of group members.
```

To state that there is a "distinct" relationship between two things doesn't tell us much. By substituting a more precise adjective, the sentence now makes a clear point:

```
There is an inverse relationship between the
socialization and selection of group members.
```

We might go one step further and revise the delayed opening ("There is . . .") of this sentence, and, in the process, eliminate a few words that contribute nothing of value.

```
The socialization and selection of group members
are inversely related.
```

2. *Uninformative words:* Avoid weak intensifiers, such as *very, really, actually,* and *certainly.* Instead, choose words that express your thoughts clearly and accurately. Thus, if something is "very important," why not describe it as "decisive," "essential," or "indispensable"? What is the difference between "*actually* being cured" and "being cured," or between "*really* confident" and "confident"? These words are fine in everyday conversation, but they aren't much help in writing social science papers.

3. *Numerical ambiguity:* Vague quantitative references often signal a need to revise for clarity. These are a particular problem in social science writing when counting is important to the story being told. In reporting that

```
Most respondents agreed that single women should
be able to obtain an abortion.
```

the obvious question arises—or ought to arise, when you read with an eye toward revising—as to how many are "most"—a little over half? two thirds? nine tenths? You can clarify this finding by substituting a more exact term for *most,* or you can explain what you mean by *most.* Here are two possible revisions:

```
Two thirds of the respondents agreed that single
women should be able to obtain an abortion.
```

```
Most respondents (67%) agreed that single women
should be able to obtain an abortion.
```

In the reporting of research findings, words such as *several, many, most, majority, few, some,* and *minority* should usually be either avoided or explained. If, however, you are discussing results that are also reported in a table, you can safely rely on these more general terms; interested readers can look to the table for more specific information.

4. *Confusing Structure:* Problems of clarity may also stem from poor organization of a sentence. Particularly in long sentences, make sure that phrases that go together are placed alongside one another.

```
Three groups, each with a different motive and
goal, led the crusade toward determinate
sentencing: prisoners, professors, and politicians.
```

A reader might anticipate some modification of "determinate sentencing" after the colon, but instead finds the "three groups" that are referred to at the beginning of the sentence. Why wait until the end of the sentence to identify these principal actors? Rewriting, we have

```
Three groups—prisoners, professors, and
politicians—each with different motives and goals,
led the crusade toward determinate sentencing.
```

If the sentence, though clearer, now seems excessively wordy, we might revise further:

```
Prisoners, professors, and politicians—each with
different motives and goals—led the crusade toward
determinate sentencing.
```

5. *Unclear Antecedent:* Ambiguous use of the pronouns *it, they,* and *them* can produce unintended and sometimes comic meanings. In a paper on halfway houses, a student wrote

```
Structuring them as closely as possible to a normal
home setting has helped the mentally ill adjust to
the environment outside of the hospital.
```

No doubt the author intended *them* to refer to halfway houses, but as this sentence is written, she is "structuring" people ("the mentally ill"), not buildings. In revising, a simple substitution of "halfway houses" for "them" will take care of the confusion.

Here is an example in which *they* leads to similar problems of ambiguity:

> Although roughly equal numbers of men and women
> work in white-collar occupations, they are more
> likely to report greater job satisfaction.

Who are happier at work, men or women? When revising, make sure that your reader can easily identify who or what you have in mind when you use *it, they, them, these,* or *those.* Even if it sounds a bit awkward, it is better to repeat whatever *it* is than to create potential ambiguities.

REVISING FOR CONCISENESS

Does each sentence make its point in the fewest words possible? Revising for content and clarity ensures that each sentence says something; revising for conciseness ensures that what you say is said well. Wordiness is probably the most frequent problem I find in papers I edit. It is undoubtedly my own worst writing problem. (By the way, in an earlier draft, the previous sentence read, "I know that it undoubtedly is the worst problem in my own writing.") Sentences can be of various lengths, but should never waste the reader's time or hinder understanding. Consider this sentence from a paper on the birth of the asylum in America:

> Definitions of social deviance, as well as ideas as
> to what the treatment of social deviants should be,
> differed greatly between the Americans of the
> Colonial period and those of the Jacksonian period,
> causing the treatment of these people to change
> dramatically.

Is the author saying that as ideas about treating deviance changed, deviants were treated differently? (Note that the vague reference to "these people" at the end of the sentence is also troubling.) It would be clearer (and obviously shorter) to write the following:

> Definitions of social deviance differed greatly between the Colonial and Jacksonian periods, resulting in a major change in how deviants were treated.

Revision may also be warranted when too little is said in too many sentences. If a series of brief statements appears repetitive, there is a good chance that a revised version with fewer sentences will leave a stronger impression. Discussing the deinstitutionalization of mental patients, a student writes the following:

> Deinstitutionalization has its roots in three philosophical ideas. These all relate to the way in which mentally ill people can be treated most effectively and humanely. These three concepts are: normalization, treatment in the least restrictive setting, and the developmental model of programming.

The tedious repetition of "these" in the second and third sentences ought to warn the writer that revision is in order. One such revision might be this:

> Deinstitutionalization is rooted in three philosophies—normalization, treatment in the least restrictive setting, and the developmental model of programming—each of which seeks the most effective and humane treatment of the mentally ill.

Although the revised sentence is relatively long, it avoids the repeated reference to the "three philosophies." One can continue to refine the sentence. Different constructions in your paper can make your ideas stand out by tailoring the thought to the appropriate pattern. For example, sometimes a strong point can be made with a short sentence. One could therefore divide the above into two sentences, the second pointing out with simple words the central reason for these complicated theories.

```
Deinstitutionalization is rooted in three
philosophies—normalization, treatment in the least
restrictive setting, and the developmental model of
programming. Each of these seeks the most effective
and humane treatment of the mentally ill.
```

Passive constructions should usually be edited out; they add words and often obscure who or what is the intended subject of the sentence. In a passive construction, the subject does not act but is acted on. "The respondent was interviewed by the researcher" is passive. (The subject of the sentence—the respondent—is acted on.) In contrast, "The researcher interviewed the respondent" is active. (The subject of the sentence—the researcher—acts.) Consider the following two sentences along with their possible revisions:

```
PASSIVE: With regard to sentencing, women criminals
are treated more favorably than their male
counterparts.

ACTIVE: The courts give lighter sentences to women
than to men.

PASSIVE: It was for the benefit of the handicapped
children that the law was brought into effect.

ACTIVE: Congress created the law to benefit
handicapped children.
```

In the first example, the subject—women criminals—is being acted on by the (implied) judicial system. In the second, "the law" is likewise acted on by some unspecified legislative body. By using active constructions, the revisions of these two sentences state un-ambiguously who or what is acting. Sometimes passive construc-tions appear repeatedly in scholarly journals; however, they should be used sparingly in college papers. One guiding point is that the passive voice is fine if the same subject, the researcher for example, is the entity repeating some action or research design.

The example about sentencing criminals illustrates another common source of wordiness: elaborate phrasing of simple terms Does it make sense to write "male counterparts" instead of "men"? Social scientists have long been criticized for inventing a language to describe everyday life in complicated terms, and expressions such as "male counterparts" only add fuel to the critics' fire. So do phrases such as "socialization process" (socialization *is* a process) or "indi-vidual norms" (*norms* are standards established and recognized by *groups*). This does not mean that you should avoid social science ter-minology altogether. Some examples of their appropriate use are dis-cussed in the following section on "Revising for Trite Expressions and Social Science Jargon."

Consider one last example that combines many of the prob-lems we have been looking at. Returning to the paper from which the last sample sentence was drawn, we read the following:

> Now that it has been discussed whether the
> nonhandicapped students will have adverse reactions
> to the mainstreaming process, those who are
> directly affected by the Act must be considered.

There are at least four ways in which this sentence can be improved through revision. First, the author is obviously trying to make a transition from one section of the paper to another, but she uses a passive construction to do so ("Now that it has been dis-cussed. . . .") Second, the vague diction of the sentence obscures its meaning. *Are* nonhandicapped students adversely affected by mainstreaming? If they are not (and that is her point), isn't it better to say, "Nonhandicapped students are not adversely affected by mainstreaming"? Third, the sentence is plagued by wordiness.

"Mainstreaming process" is used where "mainstreaming" would suffice, and "those who are directly affected by the Act" is a needlessly complicated synonym for "handicapped children." Fourth, the sentence ends with another passive construction ("those . . must be considered"). Searching for a clear and concise path out of this mess, we might revise the sentence in the form of a question:

```
If mainstreaming does not adversely affect
nonhandicapped students, how does mainstreaming
affect the handicapped?
```

The phrase "Now that is has been discussed" is one of several "academic passives" (Barnet and Stubbs 1995) that, sad to say, often crop up in scholarly writing. Most academic passives are some variation on "It has been found/demonstrated/discussed/argued/shown" or "In this paper it has been found/demonstrated. . . ." However, for undergraduate writing particularly, don't thrust the responsibility for what you write onto the paper itself; instead, identify the source. If you are the one "finding, demonstrating, or showing," simply write "I found," "I demonstrated," or "I showed." If others deserve the credit, name them: "The instructor found," "Cloward and Ohlin (1966) argued. . . ." Acknowledging the source of each statement will help you avoid passive constructions and unintentional plagiarism at the same time.

REVISING FOR TRITE EXPRESSIONS AND SOCIAL SCIENCE JARGON

Trite Expressions

Does any sentence contain trite expressions? In contrast to sentences written in the passive voice, which often convey a sense of pretentious formality, trite phrases make your writing too familiar and cloud intended meanings. To instructors, they often indicate a hastily written paper. What do the authors of the following sentences have in mind?

```
Not all juvenile delinquents go on to pursue a life
of crime.
```

```
Telephone interviewing is a quick and dirty way to
collect survey data.
```

What does the author of the first sentence mean by "a life of crime"? Is she saying that most juvenile delinquents grow up to be lawful citizens? That most juvenile delinquents (who, as a group, commit less serious crimes) fail to become adult offenders (who, as a group, commit more serious crimes)? That most delinquents are not recidivists? Similarly, what does the second author mean when she describes telephone interviewing as "quick and dirty"? Does she mean that it is "inexpensive," "expedient," or "efficient", or is she suggesting that telephone interviewing produces less reliable or less valid information than other methods of data collection? As they are written, it is impossible to know what the creators of these sentences intended to convey to their readers. To be frank, inexact and hackneyed expressions can even offend professors, who have worked carefully to define and critically evaluate concepts in their field.

Jargon

Does any sentence contain jargon? Are social science terms used vaguely or incorrectly? Some social science terms have been incorporated into everyday language and, in the process, have lost their precise and intended meanings. Many of these terms have become infused with present day controversies, such as the word "liberal" in political science or economics. When authors of social science papers misuse such terms, their writing suffers. Two of the most frequently misused social science terms appear in the following sentences:

```
Due to the bureaucracy of the organization, I was
unable to obtain the average age or average length
of employment for each group of workers.
```

```
The fieldwork experience left me feeling quite
alienated.
```

The word *bureaucracy* has a specific meaning in the social sciences; it refers to organizations with hierarchical structures of authority in which relationships among members are based on position and in which formal rules dictate how things are done. In the first example, the author uses *bureaucracy* to mean the ways in which members shift responsibility to others, making it difficult to obtain information (i.e., equivalent to the negative expression "red tape"). At least this is what I *think* she means. Without identifying exactly what aspect of bureaucracy created the problem, the statement is ambiguous.

In the second example, it is almost impossible to decipher the author's intention in describing her experience as "alienating." An informed reader might first ask *what* the writer is alienated from (work, others, or self?) and then wonder what dimension of alienation the writer has in mind (powerlessness, meaninglessness, isolation?). In short, concepts such as alienation and bureaucracy have firmly established meanings in the social sciences; to use them casually reveals a lack of understanding of these meanings. (Another frequently misused concept is "charisma." Students often describe someone with a dynamic and captivating personality as "charismatic." As a social science concept, it refers to a type of authority or leadership ability based on a person's extraordinary personal characteristics.)

Does this mean that you should always delete social science terminology from your writing? Certainly not. When properly used, technical terms can be word-saving devices that allow you to write clearly and concisely. Consider the following observations:

```
Acquiring a peculiar vocabulary is often essential
to how individuals learn to think and behave in
accordance with group values and norms.
```

What if the author had written the following instead:

```
Acquiring a peculiar vocabulary is often an
essential aspect of socialization.
```

Students of sociology know that *socialization* may be defined as "how individuals learn to think and behave in accordance with group values and norms." The writer knows that they are familiar with the meaning of "socialization," and so she uses the word in the interest of conciseness. The revision preserves the meaning of the original sentence and does so in considerably fewer words. The key here is knowing whether your audience will easily understand the terms as you comprehend them.

One final note: Don't blame *society* for everything. Whenever I read through a stack of student papers or examinations, I am overwhelmed by the power of *society* to shape human behavior: "Society encourages people to want things they can't afford"; "Society is responsible for our drug problem today"; "Society rewards conforming behavior." Although (to paraphrase Emile Durkheim) society is obviously more than the mere sum of its parts, don't fall into the habit of reifying it. Used indiscriminately, *society* becomes a vehicle for sloppy social science writing (and thinking).

As you reread a sentence that contains the word *society,* ask yourself: Whom or what do I mean by *society?* Quite often, you can replace *society* with a more specific subject: "Advertisements encourage people to want things they can't afford"; "People take drugs to avoid the responsibilities of everyday life"; "Parents and teachers reward conforming behavior among children." If you remember to state your observations concretely, you will become a better analyst of social life. At the same time, you will spare your reader some confusion. To return to an earlier caveat, journal articles do not always follow the rules on jargon or polemical terms, but you will do well to keep your writing as clear and as disciplined as possible.

REVISING FOR SPELLING ERRORS

Is every word spelled correctly? Edit with a dictionary at your side, or use a word processor with a spell-checking program. If you don't own one, buy a dictionary the next time you are in your college bookstore. (Look for *Webster's Collegiate Dictionary, Webster's New World Dictionary,* or *The American Heritage Dictionary.*) Papers submitted without having been edited for clarity and conciseness pose problems in and of themselves; misspelled words magnify these shortcomings. Your reader may be sympathetic to your difficulty in presenting ideas using the correct words, as long as whatever words you choose are at least spelled correctly. But if your paper reveals that you have not even bothered to check the spelling of a word, you will probably lose your reader's goodwill. With the advent of sophisticated spelling programs, a higher standard is expected of all writers, with the paradoxical problem of computers not finding diction (wrong word but correct spelling) errors. One of my students called communist North Korea a "rouge" (French for red) rather than a "rogue" (outlaw) state. The computer could not understand or identify the unintended pun; the word was correctly spelled. Only human revision can identify what the program cannot.

Although all of us have words we seldom spell correctly, many students find the following words particularly troublesome:

INCORRECT	CORRECT
devient, devience	deviant, deviance
respondant	respondent
defendent	defendant
signifigant, signifigance	significant, significance
socialogy (disturbing!)	sociology
indispensible	indispensable
questionaire	questionnaire
enviornment	environment
bureacracy	bureaucracy
Gemeinshaft, Gessellshaft	Gemeinschaft, Gesellschaft

Notice that the first six words in this list contain the *schwa*—the unstressed vowel that sounds like "uh." Such words are often difficult to spell because of the ambiguity of which vowel sounds like "uh." Is it "indispensible," "indispenseble," or "indispensable"? Don't guess; look up words such as these until you are sure which vowel is correct.

Your instructor will probably be annoyed if you misspell terms or names that are discussed in course materials, such as the name of the discipline. If an instructor corrects your spelling on one paper, don't make the mistake of misspelling the same word on later assignments. As mentioned in Chapter 1, compiling a list of previous mistakes will result in more efficient revision. In particular, always check the spelling of proper nouns. There is only one *b* in Max Weber's name; Goffman's first name is Erving, not Irving; Alexis *de* Tocqueville, not Alexis D'Tocqueville, wrote *Democracy in America.* Foreign names or countries require particular scrutiny; Russian words for example cannot be spelled as they sound. Your instructor may not expect you to memorize the spelling of every term or individual mentioned in a course, but misspelling important words on a class assignment will give the impression that you haven't bothered to check the accuracy of your class notes.

REVISING FOR GRAMMAR AND PROPER WORD USAGE

Because a comprehensive discussion of editing for grammatical errors would easily fill a third of this book, I will mention only a few of the recurrent problems in the student papers I read. (For a detailed examination of subject–verb agreement, parallel construction, punctuation, and other matters of grammar, I suggest you consult these excellent references: Barnet and Stubbs [1995]; Maimon, Belcher, Hearn, Nodine, and O'Connor [1981]; Strunk and White [2000]; and Zinsser [1988]. Complete citations for these books are located in the references at the end of this book.) First, I discuss run-on sentences and comma faults, which pose particular problems for students. Next, I focus on four examples of proper usage that require particular attention. Please remember that the reader may fail to grasp your insights if you write carelessly. Proper usage and grammar are as vital as the substance of the paper.

1. *Run-on sentences and comma faults.* Run-on sentences result from writing as though you do not need punctuation to separate independent clauses; comma faults (or comma splices) occur when you decide that a comma (or semicolon), rather than a period, will correct the problem of writing run-on sentences.
Run-on sentence:

> Richardson's (1995) methodology has been challenged however no one has replicated his study.

Comma fault:

> Richardson's (1995) methodology has been challenged, however no one has replicated his study.

Be on the lookout for run-on sentences and comma faults in sentences that contain transitional words (e.g., *however, instead, nevertheless, consequently,* and *thus*) or in long sentences of any kind. Following the advice of Barnet and Stubbs (1995), you have at least five options in revising these grammatical mistakes. Repairing sentences can lead to further benefits. Notice how each sentence model conveys ideas in distinct ways and can lend variety to your writing:
a. Use a period to separate the two independent clauses into two sentences.

> Richardson's (1995) methodology has been challenged. No one, however, has replicated his study.

(Note that I have placed *however* after *no one* in the revision to emphasize the contrasting information of the second sentence. This does not, however, affect the grammatical solution I suggest.)

b. Use a semicolon.

> Richardson's (1995) methodology has been
> challenged; no one, however, has replicated his
> study.

c. Use a comma and a coordinating conjunction (e g., *and, or, not, but, yet*).

> Richardson's (1995) methodology has been
> challenged, yet no one has replicated his study.

d. Use a subordinating conjunction (e.g , *although, because, unless, when, after*), and make one of the independent clauses subordinate to the other.

> Although Richardson's (1995) methodology has been
> challenged, no one has replicated his study.

e. Change one of the independent clauses to a word or phrase. (Note that I have altered the subject of the first clause in making this revision.)

> Richardson's (1995) study has been challenged on
> methodological grounds but not replicated.

2. *Which/that.* These two words are not interchangeable. *Which* introduces a nonrestrictive clause, an idea or some information that is not essential to the meaning of the sentence. *That,* in contrast, begins a restrictive clause, one that, if omitted, changes the meaning of the sentence.

> Schools that disregard federal guidelines for
> recruiting minority students are denied government
> funding.

> This school, which disregarded guidelines for
> recruiting minority students, was denied government
> funding.

The first sentence narrows or restricts the subject from "schools" to a certain group of schools—"schools that disregard federal guidelines." That is, it defines under what conditions schools will be denied funding; the meaning of the sentence would be changed significantly if the restrictive clause beginning with *that* were removed (i.e., "Schools are denied government funding"). In the second sentence, in contrast, the subject is now narrowed or restricted. The subject is simply "this school." The sentence retains its original meaning if the nonrestrictive clause beginning with *which* is omitted (i.e., "This school was denied government funding"). The nonrestrictive clause does, however, provide additional information about the particular school that was denied funding.

Notice that in the second sentence the clause beginning with *which* is set off by commas. Whenever a clause contains a parenthetical remark or an aside (and therefore must be set off by commas in order to make sense), use *which*.

3. *Effect/affect.* As a noun, effect means "result":

> The interviewer's sex had an effect on the response to this question.

Effect, as a verb, means "to bring about":

> The interviewer's sex effected a change in the response to this question.

Affect is usually used as a verb meaning "to influence":

> The interviewer's sex affected the response to this question.

Sometimes, particularly in psychological writing, affect is used as a noun meaning "feeling," "emotion," or "desire":

> Although child abuse is a highly emotional issue, the subjects showed little affect in discussing it.

4. *Using i.e./e.g.* Don't confuse *i.e.* (an abbreviation for the Latin *id est,* "that is") with *e.g.* (an abbreviation of *exempli gratia,* "for example"). Use *i.e.* when you provide another way of saying something you have written; use *e.g.* to give one or more illustrations of something you have written. Here are two examples where *i.e.* is appropriate:

> We selected respondents using a systematic random sampling technique—i.e., beginning with a random start, every fifth person was selected from a list of all community residents.

> No one involved in the research (i.e., professors, confederates, or subjects) anticipated the results of the simulated prison experiments.

In the first example, the independent clause following "i.e." provides detailed information about what the author means by "a systematic random sampling technique." In the second example, the parenthetical phrase specifies precisely who the author had in mind when writing "no one." In both sentences, the words preceding "i.e." and those following "i.e." are equivalent; they could have been switched without changing the meaning of the sentence.

When your goal is to illustrate rather than restate, use *e.g.* Here is an example in which *e.g.* is used appropriately:

> Typologies depicting changes in the dominant forms of social organization (e.g., Toennies's Gemeinschaft and Gesellschaft, Marx's "feudal" and "capitalistic," Maine's "status" and "contract") are an important part of the intellectual tradition of the social sciences.

Toennies, Marx, and Maine were not the only social theorists who described the changes in collective life associated with the passing of the Middle Ages. The student might well have added Durkheim, Weber, Redfield, Cooley, and Parsons to the list following "e.g." These additional references, however, are not necessary; the information following "e.g." is meant to be illustrative, not exhaustive. You simply want to give your reader a better idea of what you are talking about by using a few well-chosen examples.

What if, in an effort to convey a sense of the quantity of available illustrations, the author had written this sentence instead? (The only change is the addition of "etc.")

```
Typologies depicting changes in the dominant
forms of social organization (e.g., Toennies's
Gemeinschaft and Gesellschaft, Marx's "feudal" and
"capitalistic," Maine's "status" and "contract,"
etc.) are an important part of the intellectual
tradition of the social sciences.
```

Because the list of examples following "e.g." is understood to be only partial, adding "etc." (an abbreviation for *et cetera*, "and so on") is inappropriate. Moreover, placing "etc." at the end of a few examples, rather than giving the reader a sense that the author can supply additional examples if asked to do so, often has the opposite effect; it leaves the reader with the impression that the author has nothing in mind. In general, avoid *etc., and so forth,* and *and so on.* If you have something to add, say it. If you don't, place a period at the end of the sentence and go on to the next one. In either case, you won't leave your reader wondering what information you might have added.

5. *Data.* The word *data* is the plural of *datum*, a piece of information or something known. When you write papers in the social sciences, you will use the word *data* quite a lot; you will probably never use the word *datum*. Always pair *data* with a plural verb (e.g., "the data *are* consistent," "the data *were* interesting," "these data *have* never been challenged").

THE BIG PICTURE: REVISING THE PAPER AS A WHOLE

If you follow these suggestions for revision, your paper should be full of sentences that are relatively meaningful, clear, concise, and free of spelling and grammatical errors But, as you know, an effective paper is more than a collection of several pages of effective sentences. In order to reap the benefits of sentence-by-sentence revision, you must think seriously about how those sentences can be used to build strong paragraphs and, in turn, a strong paper. Before you submit your paper, review this list of issues that address revisions of your paper as a whole. (By its nature, this type of revising cannot be illustrated on a sentence-by-sentence basis. I therefore refer you to previous sections of this book for help in making revisions that concern the paper in general.)

1. *Beginnings.* Does your introduction accurately and clearly state the thesis of your paper? Introductions and conclusions are critical elements of any paper. Your readers will expect the first few paragraphs of your paper to tell them, briefly and in an organized way, what will follow. Always consider the audience. Will they understand where you are going from the start of the paper? Try to capture your reader's interest with your introduction—begin with an interesting example or analogy, or tantalize your reader by hinting at your conclusions—but at the very least, present the major issues you will address in your paper (see Chapter 4).

2. *Endings.* Does your conclusion do more than summarize your paper? Use the conclusion of your paper to go beyond a restatement of your thesis ("In this paper, I have shown X, Y, and Z"). Demonstrate the broader significance of your argument by providing analogous illustrations; suggest some questions that remain unanswered by your analysis; or emphasize the novel approach or interpretation you have made in your paper. Remember that the points you make here will be the most likely to influence the interpretation of your work. Be certain, however, that you set the stage for your concluding remarks; the conclusion of your paper is no place to introduce entirely new arguments or evidence (see Chapter 4).

3. *Organization.* Does your paper tell a logical story; that is, does it move in an orderly way from one point to another? Is similar information grouped together, or is it scattered throughout your paper?

One way to improve the organization of a paper is to write from an outline (see Chapter 5), but often you can improve a paper's organization by simply asking about each sentence (after the first): Does this sentence follow from the previous sentence? If so, how does it follow it? Does each paragraph clearly expand on the central idea of the work?

4. *Consistency.* Is the tone of your paper consistent? If you begin your paper using formal language, do you maintain that tone? Is your choice of verb tense consistent; for example, if you have been describing your research methodology in past tense, do you present your results using the same tense? Do citations of research materials follow a consistent format? (See Chapter 7 on citation form.)

5. *Balance.* What is the balance between description and analysis in your paper? Most social science papers are analyses, and you should devote more time to analysis than to description. Do you have enough evidence to support the points you are making, or do you have too much evidence? In a qualitative analysis based on interview data, for example, two carefully selected quotations from respondents are preferred over five quotations that provide redundant evidence for the same point. Finally, what is the balance between quotation and summary in your paper? Is every quotation well chosen and important to your analysis? (See Chapter 5 and Chapter 7 on when and how to use quotations.)

6. *Emphasis.* Are the major points of your paper clearly distinguishable from the minor points? If your paper is sufficiently long, consider using subheadings to divide it into major sections (see Chapter 5). Emphasis can also be established by repetition or summary; returning to an issue a few times in your paper will demonstrate its significance to your reader.

7. *Transitions.* Does your paper include proper transitions (e.g., "furthermore," "on the other hand," "however") as you move from one paragraph or one point to another? Is it clear when you are making a point of comparison or contrast? Well-placed transitions minimize the choppiness of your writing and strengthen an analysis employing comparisons (e.g., "similarly," "in addition to," "moreover") or differences (e.g., "nonetheless," "although," "in contrast").

PUTTING IT ALL TOGETHER: AN EDITOR'S GUIDE

Here is one guide I have found helpful in structuring the editing process. Although it is written as a set of questions directed toward "the author," you should be able to use this guide when revising your own work, as well as that of others.

*An Editor's Guide**

1. *Statement of thesis.* Read the opening of the paper (the title, the first sentence, the first paragraph). Is the introduction effective? Does it grab your attention and also let you know where the author is going? If so, explain (in the margin) what makes it good. If not, suggest a possible improvement.

What is the author's thesis? Is it clear? Does it seem immediately reasonable? If the thesis does not seem reasonable, was the writer astute enough to realize this, and to assure you that he or she would go on to make it reasonable?

2. *First time through.* Finish reading the paper. Does the author support a consistent thesis, or are several ideas competing for attention? Jot down your impressions after this first reading. On balance, was the paper well written? Also, make a note of any major mechanical or stylistic weaknesses you found troubling. Was the author able to state complex points in a clear way, or define confusing terms?

3. *Second time through.* This time, consider the following questions as they apply to each paragraph:

What is the main point of this paragraph?

Is the main point easy to find?

*This guide draws heavily from one developed by members of The Writing Program, University of California, Los Angeles.

Is the main point reasonable?

Does the author provide adequate evidence for each argument?

Are there adequate details and examples?

Are there paragraphs needing more development or support?

Look at the transitions (e.g., "therefore," "on the other hand," "furthermore") both between paragraphs and within them. Are more transitions or more accurate transitions needed? Are the kinds of transitions all the same or do they vary? The paragraphs should not read like a tedious list of information but build explicitly on previous ones.

Is the conclusion effective? If so, explain what makes it good. Are there loose ends in the argument that need to be tied up? Is the conclusion anticlimactic or, conversely, does it mention a major idea not explored earlier in the paper? If so, suggest a possible improvement.

4. *Third time through.* On this last reading look for two things: tone and style. Does the author know his or her audience? Does he or she maintain a consistent, credible tone throughout? Is the level of diction (not only word choice but also sentence structure) consistent with the dominant tone? Do the constructions of the paper follow the same uninspired patterns, such as endless compound sentences of the same length?

Concentrate on those mechanical or stylistic problems you found particularly distressing. Consider grammar (e.g., punctuation, subject–verb agreement), spelling, wordiness, use of parallel structure, and other stylistic matters that make the paper difficult to read. Mark at least two representative sentences that require revision, and suggest ways to revise them.

Use this guide as a flexible standard, modifying it to serve your needs best. You will have to identify fairly quickly the major problems of the paper and to focus your efforts there. Similarly, if you are editing a long paper, you would edit one section or subsection of the larger piece at a time. It would not make sense to edit a 50-page paper in the manner outlined here. Above all, seek to combine some elements of sentence-by-sentence editing with some attention to overall revisions—rethinking or restructuring—of any paper you edit.

Learning to write carefully researched, well-crafted papers is one of the most lasting gifts of education. Not only will students advance in their understanding of the social sciences by the act of writing, but they will learn how to think and reason in a systematic way. As educated citizens living in complex cultures, they will question assertions made without proof and examine social issues with rigor and creative analysis. Writers at all levels and disciplines also learn enduring truths about themselves through increasing self-reflection and objectivity. Constructing a cogent argument or explaining a research methodology hones the mind and prepares students for the intellectual and personal challenges they will face in or out of academia. If there is one activity that is truly transforming, it is that act of sustained thinking we call writing.

REFERENCES

■ ■ ■

Alaska Statehood Commission.1982. *More Perfect Union: A Preliminary Report of the Alaska Statehood Commission.* Juneau, AK: Alaska Statehood Commission.

American Psychological Association. 1994. Publication Manual of The American Psychological Association. Washington, DC: American Psychological Association.

Archer, Melanie and Judith R. Blau. 1993. "Class Formation in Nineteenth-Century America: The Case of the Middle Class." Pp. 17–41 in *Annual Review of Sociology,* Vol. 19, edited by Judith Blake and John Hagan. Palo Alto, CA: Annual Reviews.

Barnet, Sylvan and Marcia Stubbs. 1995. *Practical Guide to Writing with Additional Readings.* New York, NY: HarperCollins.

Becker, Howard S. 1963. *Outsiders: Studies in the Sociology of Deviance.* New York: Free Press.

—— 1986. *Writing for Social Scientists.* Chicago, IL: University of Chicago Press.

Cuba, Lee J. 1984. "Reorientations of Self: Residential Identification in Anchorage, Alaska." Pp. 219–237 in *Studies in Symbolic Interaction,* Vol. 5, edited by Norman K. Denzin. Greenwich, CT: JAI Press.

Gerth, H. H. and C. Wright Mills, eds. 1976. *From Max Weber: Essays in Sociology.* New York, NY: Oxford University Press.

Homans, George C. 1950. *The Human Group.* New York, NY: Harcourt, Brace and Company.

Kanter, Rosabeth Moss. 1972. *Commitment and Community.* Cambridge, MA: Harvard University Press.

Kitsuse, John I. 1962. "Societal Reaction to Deviant Behavior." *Social Problems* 9:247–256.

Lindsay, Paul and William E. Knox. 1984. "Continuity and Change in Work Values among Young Adults: A Longitudinal Study." *American Journal of Sociology* 89:918–931.

Lofland, Lyn H. 1985. *A World of Strangers: Order and Action in Urban Public Space.* Prospect Heights, IL: Waveland Press.

Maimon, Elaine P., G. L. Belcher, G. W. Hearn, B. F. Nodine, and F. W. O'Connor. 1981. *Writing in the Arts and Sciences.* Glenview, IL: Scott, Foresman.

Schuman, Howard, Charlotte Steeh, and Lawrence Bobo. 1985. *Racial Attitudes in America: Trends and Interpretations.* Cambridge, MA: Harvard University Press.

Strunk, William, Jr. and E. B. White, 2000. *The Elements of Style.* New York, NY: Macmillan.

Suttles, Gerald D. 1968. *The Social Order of the Slum: Ethnicity and Territory in the Inner City.* Chicago, IL: University of Chicago Press.

Sykes, Gresham M. and David Matza. 1957. "Techniques of Neutralization: A Theory of Delinquency." *American Sociological Review* 22:664–670.

Vaughan, Diane. 1986. *Uncoupling: Turning Points in Intimate Relationships.* New York, NY: Oxford University Press.

Western, Bruce. 1995. "A Comparative Study of Working-Class Disorganization: Union Decline in 18 Advanced Capitalist Countries." *American Sociological Review* 60:179–201.

Williamson, John B. and Kathryn M. Hyer. 1975. "The Measurement and Meaning of Poverty." *Social Problems* 22:652–663.

Yarrow, Marion Radke, Charlotte Green Schwartz, Harriet S. Murphy, and Leila Calhoun Deasy. 1955. "The Psychological Meaning of Mental Illness in the Family." *Journal of Social Issues* 11:12–24.

Zinsser, William. 1988. *On Writing Well: An Informal Guide to Writing Nonfiction.* New York, NY: Harper & Row.

ACKNOWLEDGMENTS

■ ■ ■

Excerpt from "Reorientation of Self: Residential Identification in Anchorage, Alaska" by Lee J. Cuba, *Studies in Symbolic Interaction*, Vol. 5, pp. 219–237 (1984). Copyright © 1984 JAI Press Inc. Reprinted by permission of JAI Press Inc.

Excerpt from p. 1644 in *Social Sciences Index*, April 1994 to March 1995. Copyright © 1994, 1955 by the H. W. Wilson Company. All rights reserved. Reprinted with permission of the H. W. Wilson Company.

Excerpt from *SSCI, Social Sciences Citation Index*, 1995 Annual, May to August 1995, Permuterm Subject Index. Reprinted by permission of the Institute for Scientific Information © 1995. All rights reserved.

Excerpt from *Dissertation Abstracts International*, Vol. 54, No. 10, April 1994, Keyword Index, p. 73A. The excerpts from dissertation titles and abstracts contained here are published with permission from University Microfilms Inc., publishers of *Dissertation Abstracts International* (copyright © 1994 by University Microfilms Inc.) and may not be produced without their prior permission. Full copies of the dissertations may be obtained by addressing your request to: University Microfilms Inc., 300 North Zeeb Rd., Ann Arbor, MI 48106 or by telephoning (toll-free) 1-800-521-3042.

Excerpt from "An Analysis of the Effect of Admission and Transfer Policies on Nursing Care Use Patterns in Continuing Care

Retirement Communities" in *Dissertatin Abstracts International,* Vol. 54, No. 10, April 1994, p. 3844–A. Copyright © 1994 by University Microfilms International. All rights reserved. Reprinted with permission.

Edited annotation, "Epstein, Richard A., Takings: Private Property, and the Power of Eminent Domain. Cambridge, Mass.: Harvard University Press. 1985" from *American Bar Foundations Research Journal,* No. 4, Fall 1985, p. 972. Copyright © 1986 by American Bar Foundation Research Journal. Reprinted with permission of The University of Chicago Press.

Student book review. Reprinted by permission of Elizabeth L. Stone.

Book review by Gerald N. Grob of *The Discovery of the Asylum: Social Order and Disorder in the New Republic* by David J. Rothman. Reprinted with permission from *Political Science Quarterly,* Vol. 87, no. 2 (1972):325–326.

Excerpt from "Class Formation in 19th Century America" by Melanie Archer and Judith R. Blau. Reproduced, with permission, from the *Annual Review of Sociology,* Volume 19, © 1993, by Annual Reviews Inc.

Excerpts of student research paper, "What is a Liberal Arts Education? Students' Views and Academic Decisions" by Sara Gaviser, Melissa Gilbert, Stephanie Jones and Ryan Ross. Reprinted with permission of the authors.

Student library research paper, "Vaclav Havel: Revolutionary Writings" by Courtney Hagen. Reprinted with permission of the author.

Essay answer to examination question. Reprinted with permission of Linda Maria Maccini.

Excerpt from p. 429 in *The Human Group* by George H. Homans. Reprinted with permission of Transaction Publishers. Copyright © 1991 by Transaction Publishers; all rights reserved.

Index

■ ■ ■